be
ntertains

Toga Hospitality
Level 5, 45 Jones Street,
Ultimo, NSW 2007, Australia.

t: 13-TOGA
w: togahotels.com.au

Published for Toga Hospitality by
True Blue Cockatoo Pty Ltd
w: bluecockatoo.com.au

Toga Team: Belinda Johnson, Caroline Ross, Jordan Hughes

Consulting Chef/Recipe Development: Sonia van de Stadt

Photography: Ken Martin

Editor: Alison Plummer

Design: Peter Metro

National Library of Australia Cataloguing-in-Publication Data

Vibe Entertains (includes index).

ISBN 978-0-9804212-1-7 (pbk.).

1. Cookery. I. Martin, Ken, II. Plummer, Alison

Title: Vibe Entertains

Dewey Number: 641.5

Printed by Tien Wah Press, Singapore.

First printed 2008.

vibe

entertains

vibe hotels

contents

sms the
invites it's
time to ■ ■ ■

...party!

The art of effortless entertaining begins with the desire to welcome friends and family into your home, whatever the occasion. Vibe Hotels know the secrets of entertaining which is why we are sharing these recipes that look great on the plate (or in the glass!) but are simple to achieve.

Now you'll know what to serve when you have friends around for drinks, plan to share a weekend lunch, throw a backyard or beach party or need to feed the hordes before the footy.

Something to celebrate? Prepare a sparkling spread, dress up for cocktails or treat your nearest and dearest to a delicious dinner.

vibehotels.com.au

... vibe hotels

sparkling
celebrations

Grab the girls, the boys or the whole gang
for some full-on fun, serving up dazzling
food to suit the mood – champagne optional.

tamarillo scallop parcels
w nori + prosciutto

3 ripe tamarillos
6 scallops, roe removed
1 sheet of nori
2 strips of prosciutto
1 tablespoon canola oil

Cut 2 slices from the centre of each tamarillo to make 6 evenly-sized pieces. Heat the canola oil in a non-stick pan, add the tamarillo slices and lightly seal the fruit over a medium heat to caramelise the sugars and soften the fruit a little. Remove the fruit and set aside.

Now add the scallops to the juices in the pan and gently sauté over medium heat until lightly golden. Remove from heat and set aside.

Use scissors to cut 6 x 1cm wide 'ribbons' of nori and slice 6 x 1.5 cm wide strips of prosciutto. Lay a nori ribbon on top of each strip of prosciutto, then place a warm scallop on top of each piece of tamarillo. Take a ribbon of nori and prosciutto and wrap around the tamarillo and scallop joining underneath the bundle.

Prep time: 25 mins   **Cooking time:** 20 mins   **Makes:** 6

Chef's tip: This dish is a cleverly balanced contrast of the savoury and salty prosciutto and nori, the sweet scallops and the sour tamarillo flavours.

To drink: Blue Pyrenees Sauvignon Blanc, Pyrenees, VIC.

bull's horn pepper gazpacho
w tequila shooters

1kg green long 'bull's horn' peppers
   (or use green capsicum)
1 tablespoon canola oil
1 large brown onion, diced
½ teaspoon both salt and pepper
1 litre chicken or vegetable stock
bouquet garni of fresh oregano
   and marjoram

Hull and roughly chop the peppers. Heat the oil in a medium-sized pan
and then add the peppers and the onion and sauté until softened and translucent
but not coloured. Add the salt and pepper, the stock and the bouquet garni
and allow to simmer for 10 minutes.

Remove from the heat and take out the herbs. Pour the mixture into a blender and
blend until smooth. Chill in the fridge and spoon into pretty dishes or bowls to serve.

Prep time: 10 mins   **Cooking time:** 15 mins   **Serves:** 6

Chef's tip: Gazpacho is a Spanish soup served chilled – a fabulous dish
for hot climates. A bouquet garni is a little muslin bag of herbs which is used
for cooking and removed before serving. Bull's horn peppers are long, curved peppers,
look for them in your supermarket.

preserved lemon fusilli
w smoked tofu + wild olives

1   300g pack of fusilli pasta
3   tablespoons extra virgin olive oil
¼ cup white wine vinegar
2   tablespoons Dijon mustard
200g wild olives
   (or the olives of your choice)
100g preserved lemons,
   chopped

200g fresh green beans,
   sliced
250g block of smoked tofu,
   chopped into chunks
½ bunch fresh thyme
1   tablespoon Murray River
   salt flakes

Cook the pasta in rapidly boiling water according to the time defined on the pack, then drain, rinse with hot water, transfer to a bowl and place in the fridge to cool.

Combine the olive oil, white wine vinegar and Dijon mustard in a bowl and whisk together to make the salad dressing. Set aside until ready to use.

In a large serving bowl combine the pasta, olives, lemons, sliced green beans and the tofu. When ready to serve toss through the olive oil dressing, garnish with fresh thyme and sprinkle the Murray River salt flakes over the top.

Prep time: 15 mins   **Cooking time:** 15 mins   **Serves:** 6-8

Chef's tip: We used a tri-coloured fusilli – look for it in delis and gourmet stores selling a wide range of dried pasta. Murray River salt flakes are pink and have a delicate flavour, find them in delis and gourmet stores – or use other salt flakes from the supermarket as a substitute.

To drink: Optimiste Chardonnay, Mudgee, NSW.

chilli vodka shots
w crystal bay prawns

180ml vodka
2 medium orange chillies,
    sliced into rings
6 green Crystal Bay prawns,
    peeled and de-veined (tails on)
1 jar of trout pearls

Select your favourite vodka, measure 180ml (6 shots) into a jug,
add the sliced chilli and refrigerate for at least 1 hour.

In a pan of salted water, poach the king prawns until cooked, drain, then thread
a skewer through the tail and body. Transfer to a plate and refrigerate.

Take 6 cold shot glasses and fill each with a shot of vodka, making sure there
are a couple of pieces of chilli in each glass. Place ½ teaspoon of trout pearls into
each shot glass and serve with a skewered prawn on top of each glass.

Prep time: 15 mins   **Cooking time:** 15 mins   **Makes:** 6

Chef's tip: Adding the trout pearls at the last minute helps to retain
their unique saltiness and also stops the vodka going cloudy. Find trout pearls at
seafood retailers and gourmet delis.

crab salad
w celery + radicchio

2 radicchio*
3 celery sticks,
    thinly sliced crossways
handful green beans, sliced
½ punnet of green sprouts of choice
250g crab meat
1 lemon, peeled and segmented
½ cup good quality mayonnaise

Select the best of the radicchio leaves to decorate around the serving plate then finely shred the remaining leaves into a bowl. Add thinly sliced half moons of celery, sliced green beans, green sprouts and toss together. Drain the crab meat by pressing in a sieve and add to the salad.

Place the salad in the centre of the leaves on the serving plate, add dollops of mayonnaise around the outside of the salad on the leaves and garnish the top with fresh lemon segments.

Prep time: 15 mins   **Serves:** 6

Chef's tip: *Radicchio has red leaves, is similar to lettuce, but has a slightly bitter flavour which complements this dish perfectly.

To drink: Blue Pyrenees Sauvignon Blanc, Pyrenees, VIC.

butter chicken
pockets w yoghurt + snow pea sprouts

marinade

1/3 cup lemon juice
2 tablespoons ground turmeric
4 tablespoons garam masala
1 tablespoon chilli flakes
1 tablespoon ground cumin
2 tablespoons freshly grated
   root ginger
5 cloves of garlic, crushed
1 tablespoon of crushed
   cardamon seeds
1 tablespoon sweet paprika

butter chicken

6 tablespoons peanut oil
2 medium brown onions,
   peeled and diced
2kg chicken thigh fillet, diced
1 cup chicken stock
2 tins crushed tomatoes
2 heaped tablespoons tomato paste
4 bay leaves
2 cinnamon quills
250ml thickened cream
6-8 mini pita pockets
1 small tub plain yoghurt
1 punnet of green snow pea sprouts

In a bowl combine all the marinade ingredients and 3 tablespoons of peanut oil and mix to form a paste. Add diced chicken, stir to coat thoroughly, cover and place in the fridge to marinate for no less than an hour or overnight if possible.

Heat remaining peanut oil in a medium pan, sauté onions and add marinated chicken, stirring continuously until lightly browned. Add stock, crushed tomatoes and tomato paste, bring to the boil then reduce to a simmer. Add bay leaves and cinnamon quills, simmer for 20 minutes, then pour in thickened cream and simmer gently for a further 15 minutes making sure it doesn't boil. Remove cinnamon quills and bay leaves.

Take a pita pocket and make a small opening in the top, place a small scoop of yoghurt in first then fill the pocket with butter chicken mix and garnish with snow pea sprouts. Continue filling the pockets and serve on a large plate.

Prep time: 15 mins   **Cooking time:** 50 mins   **Serves:** 6-8

Chef's tip: Using a slotted spoon to fill the pockets will ensure that you don't get too much sauce in the pockets, making them too wet.

To drink: Kirrihill Companions Rosé, Clare Valley, SA.

beetroot
cured salmon
+ watercress salad

3 medium raw beetroot, peeled
100g table salt
400g fresh Atlantic salmon fillets,
  skin on
2 bunches watercress

1 medium zucchini
2 Lebanese cucumbers
75ml mirin*
75ml rice wine vinegar*
2 tablespoons palm sugar

Grate the beetroot into a bowl, add the salt and stir through. Place salmon fillets skin side down onto a sheet of plastic wrap. Press beetroot and salt mix on the flesh side of the salmon and wrap the plastic tightly around the fish. Refrigerate overnight or a minimum of 12 hours.

When you are ready to cook, remove fish from the plastic and wipe off beetroot with a clean cloth rinsed in ice-cold water. Use a knife to cut very thin slices across the fillets and keep in the fridge while you make the salad.

Wash watercress and vegetables. Pick off the end shoots and leaves of the watercress and place in a bowl, discarding the stalks. Cut zucchini into long, thin strips, leaving the skin on and use a peeler to make long thin slices of cucumber. Add to the watercress and toss together.

Dissolve the sugar in a saucepan with rice wine vinegar and mirin and allow to cool.

When ready to serve, gently toss the salmon slices with the salad, reserving a few to garnish the top of the salad. Place in a serving bowl and pour over dressing just before serving.

Prep time: 35 mins + marinating time   **Cooking time:** 10 mins   **Serves:** 6-8

Chef's tip: *Mirin is a Japanese rice wine, similar to sake. Rice wine vinegar is an Asian style vinegar – both are available at supermarkets and Asian grocers.

To drink: Rolling Sauvignon Blanc Semillon, Central Ranges, NSW.

frangelico chocolate mousse
w mandarin

2 mandarins, peeled
480g dark chocolate
120g unsalted butter
220g caster sugar
6 eggs, whites and yolks separated
125ml Frangelico liqueur
375ml thickened cream

Divide mandarins into segments, slice each into thirds, de-seeding as necessary and set aside. In a heatproof dish, melt the chocolate and butter in a bowl over simmering water until smooth, set aside.

In a separate bowl, whisk caster sugar and egg yolks until pale in colour. Add the Frangelico and whisk for a further minute. Heat this mixture over simmering water, whisking continuously until the mixture begins to thicken slightly and falls from the whisk in smooth ribbons. Stir the chocolate into the mix and set aside to cool.

Whisk egg whites until they form soft peaks and fold through the cooled chocolate then whip the cream until it also forms soft peaks and fold through the mousse mix.

Pour half of the mousse into 6 serving glasses then add a layer of chopped mandarin segments. Pour over remaining mousse and chill for 30 minutes or until ready to serve.

Garnish with fresh mandarin pieces or dipped in toffee as in the photo.
See page 146 for toffee recipe.

Prep time: 40 mins   **Cooking time:** 10-12 mins   **Serves:** 6

To drink: Tintilla Edwardo Fortified Semillon, Hunter Valley, NSW.

golden meringues
w strawberries + kiwi fruit

6 egg whites
1 pinch cream of tartar
1 pinch salt
300g caster sugar
200ml thickened cream
½ teaspoon vanilla essence
3 kiwi fruit
½ punnet strawberries

Preheat oven to 110°C. Whisk egg whites with cream of tartar and salt until they form soft peaks. Continue to whisk, gently adding the sugar until the egg whites become stiff but not dry.

On a baking sheet lined with greaseproof paper, place 16 individual dessert spoons of egg white. (You may have enough mixture to make more.) Place in the oven for 1 hour, then check to see if the meringues have dried and turned golden. If they are not golden, leave them for a further 20 minutes. Remove from the oven and cool on a rack.

Beat thickened cream and vanilla in a bowl until stiff. Remove the skin from kiwi fruit and slice into half rounds. Hull strawberries and cut into quarters. To serve, place a heaped teaspoon of cream on top of each and garnish with slices of strawberry and kiwi fruit.

Prep time: 25 mins   **Cooking time:** 1-1½ hrs   **Serves:** 12-16

To drink: Shaw Vineyard Estate Botrytis Semillon, Murrumbateman, NSW.

tropical delights

The tastes of the tropics are fresh
and tantalising with an exotic twist,
made for a laid-back beach party or chilling
out in the backyard at any time of day.

prawn skewers
w wasabi gnocchi + lime

3 medium desiree potatoes,
  skin on
1 egg
1 teaspoon wasabi
½ teaspoon salt
1 cup plain flour

extra flour for rolling
24 green Crystal Bay prawns,
  peeled and de-veined, tails on
2 large limes
1 cup good quality mayonnaise

Preheat oven to 180°C and bake potatoes until soft in the centre when skewered. Cut potatoes in half, scoop flesh into a bowl and discard skins. Mash well and add beaten egg, wasabi, salt and ¾ of the flour then knead to form a scone-like dough. Add more flour as required until dough is dry and elastic but not crumbly. (As all potatoes are different sizes the amount of flour required will vary.)

Break dough into tennis ball size pieces and roll into long sausage shapes about 3cm round on a floured surface. Use a scraper or knife to chop dough at 3cm intervals to form gnocchi pieces. This amount will give you approximately 24 pieces.

Bring a medium pot of salted water to the boil. Add gnocchi pieces and wait for them to float to the surface of the water then simmer for 2 minutes to cook flour. Remove, drain and cool on a sheet of greaseproof paper.

Blanch prawns in a pot of salted boiling water for 2 minutes, then drain. Thread prawns on to long skewers and top with a gnocchi piece. To serve, cut limes in half lengthways, removing the flesh. Arrange skewers into the top of 2 of the lime halves and fill the other 2 with mayonnaise.

Prep time: 40 mins   **Cooking time:** 15 mins   **Serves:** 6-12

Chef's tip: You need to make the gnocchi yourself in order to achieve the wasabi colour and flavour. If you make more gnocchi than you need or would like to make it in advance, you can freeze it in an airtight container.

To drink: Rolling Sparkling Pinot Grigio Chardonnay, Central Ranges, NSW.

rambutan salad
w pork + mint

6 rambutans*
1 teaspoon lemon juice
2 tablespoons peanut oil
1 small Spanish onion,
   peeled and finely chopped
2 kaffir limes leaves,
   very finely shredded
250g pork mince
Juice of 2 limes

2 tablespoons fish sauce
6 spring onion stalks,
   finely chopped
1 teaspoon sambal oelek
½ cup mint leaves,
   roughly chopped
½ cup coriander leaves,
   roughly chopped

Halve the fresh rambutans and scoop out the flesh, removing the seed from the middle. Roughly dice the flesh and set aside. Place the rambutan skins in a bowl of cold water with a teaspoon of lemon juice while you are making the pork mix to prevent the insides of the skins from going brown.

In a frying pan, heat peanut oil and add onion, shredded lime leaf and pork mince, stirring with a wooden spoon until the mince turns a golden brown. Now add lime juice, fish sauce, spring onions, sambal oelek and bring back to a simmer before removing from the heat. Allow to cool for 5 minutes before adding the mint leaves, coriander and rambutan flesh. Stir well and place into a bowl to keep in the fridge until ready to serve.

Remove the rambutan skins from the water and pat dry. Place scoops of the pork mixture into each rambutan skin and arrange on a plate to serve.

Prep time: 15 mins   **Cooking time:** 10 mins   **Serves:** 6-12

Chef's tip: *Rambutans are a tropical fruit native to south east Asia, also grown in tropical Australia, in season from October to June. This style of salad flavoured with fish sauce and lime is known as larb and originates from Laos.

To drink: Tintilla Angus Semillon, Hunter Valley, NSW.

tempura vegetables
w spicy dhal

dhal
- 1 cup red lentils
- 3 cm fresh ginger, grated
- 2 bay leaves
- 1 cinnamon stick
- 40g butter
- 1 medium brown onion, diced
- 2 garlic cloves crushed
- 1 tablespoon ground turmeric
- 1 teaspoon ground cumin
- 1 teaspoon garam masala
- Juice of ½ a lemon
- ½ tsp salt

tempura batter
- ½ cup plain flour
- ½ cup rice flour
- ½ tsp baking powder
- 1 egg
- 300ml soda water

- 2 litres of peanut oil

vegetables such as:
- 6 asparagus spears trimmed
- 6 button mushrooms
- 6 strips of eggplant
- 1 bunch of broccolini
- 6 strips of zucchini
- 1 bunch trimmed Dutch carrots

Cover lentils with cold water and soak overnight. Rinse and drain lentils and place in a medium size pot with 3 cups of water, ginger, bay leaves and cinnamon. Bring to the boil and simmer for 10-12 mins or until the lentils are soft. Remove from the heat when cooked and set aside.

In a medium frying pan add butter and diced onion and sauté until soft. Add garlic, spices and lemon juice to the pan and gently heat for 2 minutes stirring continuously to allow the spices to heat and release their flavours. Remove bay leaves and cinnamon before adding lentils to the pan, then stir well.

In a large pot bring 2 litres of peanut or your preferred cooking oil to a hot frying temperature (approx 180°C). Sift flours and baking powder together into a clean, chilled bowl. Add beaten egg and soda water and combine with a whisk. Dip trimmed vegetables into the batter a few pieces at a time and carefully place into the hot oil. They will rise to the surface and should be removed when they are lightly golden. Drain on some paper towel to remove any excess oil. Keep the pieces warm in the oven (80-100°C) while you cook the other pieces. Serve on a large plate with a side bowl of dhal for dipping.

Prep time: 20 mins   **Cooking time:** 35 mins   **Serves:** 6-8

To drink: Tintilla Rosato di Jupiter Sangiovese Rosé, Hunter Valley, NSW.

smoked fish kedgeree
w egg + parsley

5 fillets smoked cod
   (or smoked haddock)
600ml water
1 medium brown onion diced
1½ teaspoon curry powder
200g basmati rice
2 tablespoons vegetable oil

30g butter
125ml thickened cream
½ bunch flat leaf parsley,
   rough chopped
6 boiled eggs, peeled
salt and pepper to taste

Place smoked cod into a pan with the water, heat and simmer for 10 minutes. Drain the water into a separate bowl and reserve for cooking the rice.

Now flake the fish and set aside. Heat the oil in a medium saucepan add onion and sauté until soft, add curry powder and stir before adding rice and 500ml of the reserved water from the fish. Bring to the boil, cover and cook for 10 minutes or until tender. Stir in the butter and thickened cream and heat gently.

When hot again, gently fold in the flaked cod and chopped parsley. Roughly chop 3 of the boiled eggs and fold into the fish mixture. Add salt and pepper to taste then spoon onto serving plates and garnish with the remaining boiled eggs, halved.

Prep time: 20 mins   **Cooking time:** 20 mins   **Serves:** 6

Chef's tip: Kedgeree originated as an Anglo-Indian dish made with flaked, smoked fish and often served for breakfast. It also makes a delicious starter or main dish for dinner.

To drink: Optimiste Chardonnay, Mudgee, NSW.

soft spring rolls
w beef, chicken or prawns

12 sheets of rice paper rounds
150g beef rump strips, cooked
1 tablespoon soy sauce
4 chicken tenderloins, cooked
1 tablespoon sweet chilli
4 cooked king prawns, peeled
1 pkt bean shoots
¼ red cabbage, finely shredded
2 Lebanese cucumbers cut into thin
   5-8cm strips

½ bunch purple basil leaves
½ bunch coriander leaves
2 carrots cut into strips
½ bunch Vietnamese mint leaves
1 punnet snow pea shoots
3 shiitake mushrooms, sliced
4 baby corn
Water

Place ingredients ready in front of you including a large bowl of fresh cold water to soak the rice paper and a clean tea towel on a chopping board for rolling.

Soak a round of rice paper in the cold water until it becomes soft, lay out on the board and place your selected ingredients in the middle. Fold the other side over the ingredients making a half moon then roll firmly. You will still have one side of the roll open with some of the ingredients sticking out for colour and decoration making the type of roll easy to identify. Serve with your favourite dipping sauces such as soy, sweet chilli or plum.

beef rolls	chicken rolls	king prawn rolls
beef strips	chicken tenderloins	king prawns
bean shoots	coriander leaves	sliced shiitake mushroom
shredded red cabbage	Vietnamese mint	baby corn
cucumber strips	carrot strips	snow pea shoots
purple basil	cucumber strips	coriander
Vietnamese mint	snow pea sprouts	bean sprouts
snow pea sprouts		

Prep time: 30 mins   **Cooking time:** 15 mins   **Serves:** 6-12

To drink: Climbing Pinot Gris, Orange, NSW.

bbq chicken salad
w mango + rocket

2 ripe mangoes
Olive oil to cook
2 cups rocket leaves
1 head soft green lettuce
1 cup sunflower sprouts

1 large red onion, peeled and sliced
1 large BBQ'd chicken
75ml balsamic vinegar
75ml olive oil

Peel and slice the mangoes. Wash the rocket and lettuce leaves, dry and place in a serving bowl with rocket, sprouts, sliced onion and mango slices. Divide the chicken into pieces and arrange on top of the salad.

Whisk together the balsamic vinegar and olive oil and dress the salad just before serving.

Prep time: 10 mins   **Serves:** 6

Chef's tip: You can use a bought BBQ chicken for this or BBQ your own. If you prefer the taste of cold, roast chicken, try this: Preheat the oven to 180°C, place a roasting chicken in a baking tray, rub the skin with a little olive oil and cook for approximately 1½ hours until skin is golden brown and juices from the centre of the chicken turn golden instead of pink when tested with a skewer. Set aside to cool.

To drink: Blue Pyrenees Chardonnay, Pyrenees, VIC.

bami goreng noodles
w pork + prawns

400g pack thin hokkien noodles
Peanut or vegetable oil for cooking
250g sliced pork
250g green Crystal Bay prawns,
   peeled and de-veined
½ bunch spring onions, sliced
2 tablespoons sambal oelek

1 tablespoon fish sauce
1 medium onion, peeled and sliced
1 small leek sliced into rings
3 cloves garlic, peeled and finely
   sliced
75ml kecap manis*
1 punnet cherry tomatoes

Soak the noodles in warm water to separate for 5 minutes and drain. Set aside.
Heat a tablespoon of oil in a wok until hot. Cook the pork and prawns in small
batches so they don't stew, remove and set aside to rest.

Heat another tablespoon of oil in the wok, add onion, leek, garlic and half the spring
onions until glossy and starting to soften. Add cooked pork and prawns, sambal oelek,
fish sauce and toss to coat. Finally, add the noodles and kecap manis and toss until all
the ingredients are hot and glossy.

Serve into individual bowls or a big serving bowl and garnish with fresh cherry
tomato halves.

Prep time: 15 mins   **Cooking time:** 15 mins   **Serves:** 6

Chef's tip: *Kecap manis is a thick Indonesian sauce similar to a sweet soy sauce
flavoured with garlic and/or star anise. Bami Goreng is a popular fried egg noodle
dish in Indonesia.

To drink: Kirrihill Companions Chardonnay Viognier, Clare Valley/Adelaide Hills, SA.

bbq barramundi in paperbark
w lemon myrtle

2 rolls paperbark* wrap
4 whole baby barramundi (ready
   cleaned and scaled)
4 lemons, sliced
20g jar lemon myrtle leaf spice
Olive oil to season
1 ball of twine

Divide the paperbark rolls into four sheets and place a barramundi on each one. Rub both sides of each fish with olive oil and sprinkle with lemon myrtle, turn the fish over and sprinkle the other side. Take the slices of lemon and place inside each fish before rolling the paperbark around the fish.

Now tie the paperbark parcels with twine at intervals to secure the fish snugly in the paperbark.

Preheat the BBQ or chargrill then place the fish on the grill and cook on each side for 10 minutes. The outside of the paperbark will blacken and smoke the fish on the inside infusing delicious smoky and lemon myrtle flavours. Cut a small slot in one of the parcels to see that the fish is cooked before taking off the BBQ.

Prep time: 15 mins   **Cooking time:** 20-30 mins   **Serves:** 6-8

Chef's tip: *Paperbark is a natural food wrap which adds a delicate, smoky flavour for BBQ fish or chicken, for example. Available at gourmet food stores such as The Essential Ingredient.

To drink: Blue Pyrenees Sauvignon Blanc, Pyrenees, VIC.

pineapple parfait
w pistachio pashmak

500ml milk
½ cup of caster sugar
1 teaspoon vanilla extract
2 tablespoons gelatine
2 x 440g tins crushed pineapple
60ml hot water
1 packet of pistachio pashmak*

Heat milk, sugar and vanilla in a saucepan to dissolve the sugar. Cool slightly. Dissolve gelatine in hot water and whisk into milk. Drain pineapple and place in a bowl with the milk mixture. Fold all ingredients together with a spoon and refrigerate for 1½ hours, stirring 3 or 4 times while setting.

When set, stir again and spoon into glasses then garnish with a handful of pistachio pashmak just before serving.

Prep time: 10 mins   **Cooking time:** 10 mins   **Serves:** 6

Chef's tip: *Pashmak is a Persian style fairyfloss available at gourmet food suppliers. Replace with other fairyfloss if you prefer.

To drink: Shaw Vineyard Estate Semi Sweet Riesling, Murrumbateman, NSW.

dee's banoffee pie
w banana + cream

1 packet granita biscuits
100g melted butter
100g butter
100g brown sugar
380ml condensed milk

2 ripe bananas, peeled and sliced
300ml thickened cream
1 teaspoon vanilla essence
3 tablespoons caster sugar

Grease a 20cm springform cake tin. Crush granita biscuits to make fine crumbs in a bowl and add melted butter. Combine well and press into the base and sides of the cake tin. Refrigerate to set.

In a saucepan combine butter and brown sugar and heat until sugar is dissolved. Add condensed milk and bring to simmer over medium heat for 10 minutes to make a smooth caramel. Do not allow to burn, reduce heat if necessary. Fold banana slices through the caramel reserving some slices for garnish. Pour into the biscuit base lined tin and refrigerate to set for an hour.

Whip thickened cream with vanilla essence and caster sugar into peaks. Cover the caramel and banana mixture with whipped cream and garnish with remaining slices of banana.

Prep time: 20 mins   **Cooking time:** 20 mins   **Serves:** 8 –12

Chef's tip: You could add either grated chocolate, crumbled Flake bar or even drizzle chocolate topping as extra garnish.

To drink: Shaw Vineyard Estate Botrytis Semillon, Murrumbateman, NSW.

alfresco
afternoons

Invite family and friends around for
indulgent long lunches, serving platters
of food to share, Mediterranean-style.
With these recipes it's all plain sailing.

antipasto baskets
w prosciutto + red peppers + olives

2 packets Mountain Bread
   flat bread (12 sheets)
¼ cup olive oil
2 sheets puff pastry
4 tablespoons pesto
6 artichoke hearts
6 slices prosciutto

24 olives, pitted
3 chargrilled red peppers
   cut into strips
6 chargrilled aubergine slices
6 marinated mushrooms
Basil leaves for garnish

Preheat oven to 180°C. Place 2 sheets of bread into muffin tin moulds and press to make a bowl shape. Brush lightly with olive oil and bake for 5 minutes until crisp. Cool and set aside.

Brush the pastry on one side with pesto and cut into 12 strips. Now join 2 pieces together with pesto side facing out and twist them. Lay all 6 twists on a baking tray and bake for 10 minutes until crisp and golden. Cool and then wrap a slice of prosciutto around each twist.

Fill each basket with a pastry twist, artichoke heart, 4 olives, slices of chargrilled red pepper, marinated mushroom and eggplant. Garnish with fresh basil leaves.

Prep time: 15 mins   **Cooking time:** 15 mins   **Serves:** 6

Chef's tip: Any sort of flat bread can be used to make your baskets. We have used the above combination of antipasto items available at any deli, however you can vary them to suit your mood.

To drink: Blue Pyrenees Brut Rosé, Pyrenees, VIC.

warm pumpkin salad
w asparagus + spinach

1 butternut pumpkin, skin removed, cut into 2-3cm chunks
¼ cup canola oil
2 teaspoons Murray River salt
1 teaspoon cracked black pepper
2 bunches trimmed asparagus spears

250g semi-dried tomatoes
250g washed baby spinach leaves
1 bunch purple basil leaves, roughly chopped
3 tablespoons extra virgin olive oil

Preheat oven to 180°C. Place chopped pumpkin on a baking tray, rub canola oil over the pieces and sprinkle with salt and pepper. Cook in the oven until pumpkin is soft and brown on the edges. Allow to cool.

Heat a frying pan with 3 tablespoons of olive oil, roughly chop asparagus spears and lightly sauté in the olive oil. Place semi-dried tomatoes and pumpkin in the pan and toss for a further minute until all ingredients are warm. Remove from heat.

In a serving bowl first place the baby spinach leaves and purple basil leaves then add the warm ingredients and gently toss together. Serve immediately.

Prep time: 15 mins   **Cooking time:** 35 mins   **Serves:** 6-8

To drink: Tintilla Rosato di Jupiter Sangiovese Rosé, Hunter Valley, NSW. You can also use this wine to make Sangria, Spain's famous red punch.

pepper crusted tuna
w coriander

½ cup cracked black pepper
2 teaspoons ground coriander seeds
4 thick tuna fillets,
   3-4 cm thick
2 tablespoons canola oil
2 Lebanese cucumbers,
   sliced

2 cups rocket leaves
1 bunch coriander leaves
1 medium red onion,
   peeled and thinly sliced
2 teaspoons sesame oil
1 lime,
   cut into wedges

Mix cracked pepper and ground coriander seeds together on a plate. Coat all sides of the tuna fillets with the mixture and set aside while you prepare the salad.

Combine cucumber slices, rocket, coriander leaves and thinly sliced onion in a bowl, toss with the sesame oil and transfer to a serving plate.

Heat a non-stick frying pan with canola oil and sear tuna fillets over a medium heat, lower heat and cook for a further 1-1½ minutes on each side. Rest for 3 minutes before slicing in half to serve on top of the salad. Garnish with lime wedges.

Prep time: 10 mins   **Cooking time:** 5-10 mins   **Serves:** 4

To drink: Kirrihill Companions Rosé, Clare Valley, SA.

ratatouille tartlets
w marjoram + fetta

3 tablespoons olive oil
1 medium red onion,
   peeled and diced
1 red capsicum, diced
1 small eggplant,
   peeled and diced
1 zucchini, diced

2 tomatoes, diced
½ teaspoon salt flakes
½ teaspoon cracked black pepper
¼ cup fresh marjoram leaves
8 savoury tartlet pastry cases
¼ cup crumbled fetta cheese

Heat olive oil in a frying pan, add onion and capsicum and toss for a minute.

Add eggplant and zucchini and cook for a further 1-2 minutes before adding diced tomatoes, salt and pepper and marjoram leaves.

Cook for a further 5 minutes to allow tomato to soften slightly to add a creamier texture to the vegetables, but do not allow the vegetables to stew.

Remove from the heat and fill the tart cases with the ratatouille mix.
Top with crumbled fetta and serve.

Prep time: 15 mins   **Cooking time:** 10 mins   **Makes:** 8

To drink: Blue Pyrenees Chardonnay, Pyrenees, VIC.

aubergine and chickpea tagine
w chicken + almonds

2 tablespoons ghee
   or clarified butter
1 large red onion, peeled and diced
1 aubergine, diced
2 tomatoes, diced
2 cans chick peas, drained
1 teaspoon paprika
1 teaspoon cumin

1 teaspoon cayenne pepper
1 teaspoon salt
750ml chicken stock
6 chicken drumettes, bone in
1 cup couscous
1 tablespoon vegetable oil
½ cup flaked almonds
1 bunch coriander, roughly chopped

In a heavy based saucepan (or tagine) melt the ghee and sauté the onion, eggplant and tomatoes until they soften. Add chickpeas and stir for a further minute. Add paprika, cumin, cayenne pepper and salt, then stir. Add 400ml of chicken stock, bring to a slow simmer and allow to soften and thicken for 30 minutes on a low heat.

While the vegetables are simmering, brown the chicken drumettes in a frying pan until golden and cooked. Place them into the tagine mix to soak up the flavours while you prepare the couscous.

In a separate saucepan, bring the remaining chicken stock to the boil. Meanwhile, place couscous in a bowl and add the vegetable oil, mixing to coat the grains. Toss flaked almonds through the couscous. Pour the boiled chicken stock over the couscous mix, but do not stir. Cover with plastic wrap to allow the grains to soak up the stock. When all the liquid has been absorbed stir the couscous with a fork to make it fluffy.

To serve, arrange the couscous on the base of a serving dish and top with the vegetable tagine and chicken pieces. Garnish with chopped coriander.

Prep time: 15 mins   **Cooking time:** 45 mins   **Serves:** 6

To drink: Optimiste Chardonnay, Mudgee, NSW.

poached snapper
w lemongrass + coconut

4　medium snapper fillets
3　stems lemongrass
2　x 400ml tins coconut cream
500ml fish stock
3　tablespoons fish sauce
1　bunch coriander
6　bok choy, trimmed
6　wedges of lime
Steamed rice to serve

Cut snapper fillets into thirds to make a total of 12 pieces. Cut lemongrass into quarters and bruise to release the flavour. In a fish poacher or a pot large enough to submerge the fish, add coconut cream, lemongrass, fish stock, fish sauce and whole bunch of coriander. Bring to a slow rolling simmer.

Meanwhile, bring a pot of water to the boil and blanch bok choy for 30 seconds then drain. Gently place fish on the inner tray of the poacher or into the pot and slowly simmer for 7 minutes per 2.5cm of fish thickness, making sure fish pieces are covered with the poaching liquid.

Remove one piece to check if the fish is cooked in the centre, if not return to the liquid for a further 2 minutes and check again. To serve, place the bok choy on a serving plate, top with poached snapper and spoonfuls of the liquid.

Prep time: 20 mins　　　**Cooking time:** 15 mins　　　**Serves:** 6

To drink: Climbing Pinot Gris, Orange, NSW.

bbq beef ribs
w roast garlic + macadamia pesto

3kg beef ribs
1 cup olive oil
3 whole garlic bulbs
1 bunch basil
200g macadamia nuts
60g shaved or grated parmesan
1 teaspoon sea salt flakes

Preheat oven to 180°C. Cut ribs into portion size pieces for 6. Slice garlic bulbs horizontally in halves and rub over beef ribs. Place ribs and garlic bulbs on a roasting tray and brush ribs with some of the olive oil. Roast in the oven for 10 minutes to help the cooking process and to soften the garlic bulbs. Remove and rest until BBQ is ready.

Place roasted macadamia nuts in food processor and pulse until nuts become a rough paste, remove and set aside. Add basil leaves to food processor with salt and 75ml of oil. Pulse to a paste. Now add parmesan, the macadamia mix and a further 75ml of olive oil and combine to form a pesto paste.

If the pesto is still slightly dry, add a little more oil until spreadable.

Preheat BBQ. Place the garlic on the slowest part of the BBQ, flat-side down and allow it to soften. Cook the ribs at the same time basting with pesto as you go for a further 10 minutes.

Reserve a portion of the pesto to spread over the ribs after cooking for presentation.

Serve with a half of soft garlic to squeeze over the ribs.

Prep time: 20 mins   **Cooking time:** 25 mins   **Serves:** 6

To drink: Optimiste Cabernet Sauvignon, Mudgee, NSW.

baked red emperor
w olives + lemon thyme

1 whole red emperor (cleaned)
3 lemons, sliced
1 bunch lemon thyme
125ml olive oil
1 red onion, peeled and quartered
250g of your favourite olives
1 tablespoon sea salt flakes

Preheat the oven to 180°C. Line a baking tray large enough to fit the fish with greaseproof paper. Prepare the fish by cutting 3 to 4 slits depending on the size of the fish from behind the head in 4cm intervals to the tail on both sides of the fish.

Place slices of lemon and sprigs of thyme into the slits on one side of the fish and rub with a little olive oil. Place this side of the fish down on the baking tray. Stuff the cavity of the fish with the ends of the lemon, onion wedges, some of the olives and a few thyme sprigs. Place more lemon and thyme into the slits on the top side of the fish and rub with a little olive oil, sprinkle with salt and scatter the remaining olives over and around the fish.

Cover the baking tray with foil and bake the fish in the oven for 20 to 30 minutes or until the flesh is white, moist and pulls away from the bones. Using the baking paper, slide the fish and the baking paper onto the serving plate. Once the fish is on the plate you can easily slide the paper from under the fish. Serve immediately with a great salad.

Prep time: 15 mins   **Cooking time:** 30 mins   **Serves:** 8

Chef's tip: For a better chance of your fish making it to the plate in one piece, use the baking paper to lift rather than trying to balance with tools. You can use another fish of your choice, such as snapper and use thyme instead of lemon thyme.

To drink: Rolling Sauvignon Blanc Semillon, Central Ranges, NSW.

strawberry sundae
w vanilla bean ice cream

2 punnets of strawberries
2 tablespoons caster sugar
75ml Cointreau or orange liqueur
75ml orange juice

500g tub of good quality
   vanilla bean or vanilla ice cream
6 mint sprigs

Chill 6 serving bowls or glasses in the fridge. Select 6 of the best strawberries to reserve for garnishing then slice half and dice the other half of the remaining strawberries.

Place into a saucepan with Cointreau, orange juice and caster sugar.

Stir ingredients and bring to a low simmer for 2 minutes. Move to a container and cool in the fridge until ready to serve.

Place 2 scoops of vanilla bean ice cream into each of the serving dishes or glasses, spoon on the strawberries and garnish each with a strawberry and a sprig of mint.

Prep time: 15 mins   **Cooking time:** 5 mins   **Serves:** 6

To drink: Shaw Vineyard Estate Botrytis Semillon, Murrumbateman, NSW.

tangelo creams
w madeira + chocolate

4 tangelos
250g Madeira cake
300ml thickened cream
1 teaspoon vanilla flavouring
3 tablespoons Dutch cocoa powder
2 tablespoons caster sugar

Slice the tops off the tangelos, about 3 cm down. Scoop out the pulp, chop it up and transfer to a bowl. Cut Madeira cake into small cubes, mix with the tangelo pulp and refrigerate.

Beat cream, vanilla, cocoa and sugar together until stiff to make the chocolate cream. When ready to serve, fill tangelo skins with the Madeira and tangelo mix to the rims and top with chocolate cream – spooning it on or piping it for a designer finish.

Prep time: 20 mins   **Serves:** 4

Chef's tip: If you want to be even more decorative you can make toffee 'nests' for the tangelos using the toffee recipe on page 146. Arrange the tangelo skins upside down on baking paper on a baking tray and drizzle with toffee syrup and cool at room temperature. If you can't find tangelos then sweet oranges also work.

To drink: Tintilla Edwardo Fortified Semillon, Hunter Valley, NSW.

drop · in for
drinks

Add modern flavours and a touch of imagination to your get-togethers. On the balcony, beside the pool, in the garden, these recipes are all you need.

chinese buns
w nashi pear + duck parfait

12 Chinese buns*
1 beaten egg
600g duck livers (or chicken livers)
1 tablespoon olive oil
1 small brown onion,
   peeled and finely diced
1 clove of garlic,
   peeled and finely diced

60ml brandy
1½ cups port
½ bunch thyme
½ teaspoon salt
½ teaspoon ground white pepper
125g unsalted butter, softened
60ml cream
3 nashi pears

Preheat oven to 180°C. Brush the Chinese buns with beaten egg and brown in oven for 10 minutes. Set aside and cover when cool. Trim the livers and set aside.

Heat a saucepan with 1 tablespoon of olive oil. Sauté diced onion and garlic until soft. Add brandy and cook for 30 seconds before adding duck livers. Sauté for a further 2 minutes. Add port, thyme, salt and pepper and simmer slowly for 20 minutes. Remove from the heat and take out the thyme sprigs.

Place into food processor with butter and cream and blend until smooth. Place the mix into a sieve and press through with the back of a wooden spoon for a smooth texture. Place in fridge to cool and set.

When ready to serve, slice nashi pear into 12 slices, 1-2 cm thick. Slice Chinese buns in half and place a slice of nashi pear on each bun. Spoon parfait on top of the nashi pear slices, replace the lid of each bun and serve.

Prep time: 20 mins   **Cooking time:** 30 mins   **Makes:** 12

Chef's Tip: Buy *Chinese Buns from bakers in Chinatown or Asian grocers. If you can't find duck livers they can be replaced with chicken livers. Nashi pears are a cross between apples and pears and are readily available at supermarkets.

salmon satay
w pickled ginger + lime mayonnaise

¼ cup pickled ginger
250ml mayonnaise
juice of 1 lime
2 Atlantic salmon fillets,
    skin removed

1 jar satay paste
1 tablespoon peanut oil
6 skewers
6 lime wedges

Roughly chop pickled ginger and place in a bowl, add mayonnaise
and lime juice and chill until ready to use.

Coat salmon steaks all over with satay paste and marinate in a bowl in
the fridge for a minimum of 20 minutes. When ready to cook, heat the oil in a
non-stick pan and sear salmon for 1 minute on either side.

Remove from the heat and allow salmon to rest for a further 5 minutes.

Slice salmon fillets into 12 cubes and place 2 cubes on each skewer.
Arrange the skewers on a serving plate with pickled ginger mayonnaise and
wedges of fresh lime on the side.

Prep time: 20 mins   **Cooking time:** 10 mins   **Makes:** 6 skewers.

Chef's tip: Satay paste, like satay dipping sauce, is a favourite made with
peanuts, tamarind, chilli, lemongrass and shrimp paste – buy it in jars from
the supermarket.

To drink: Shaw Vineyard Estate Vive Spritzy White, Murrumbateman, NSW.

seared chicken tenderloins
w dukkah

dukkah:
100g pistachios
50g hazelnuts blanched
50g macadamias
1 tablespoon sea salt flakes
1 teaspoon cumin powder
½ teaspoon cayenne pepper
1 tablespoon sesame seeds

8 chicken tenderloins
100ml extra virgin olive oil
100ml balsamic glaze
(available at supermarkets)

Preheat oven to 150°C. On a dry baking sheet, roast pistachio, hazelnut and macadamia nuts for 5 minutes or until golden. Keep an eye on them as they can burn quite quickly. Remove from the oven and cool. When cool, pulse the nuts in a food processor for a coarse chop then place in a bowl and combine with salt flakes, cumin powder, cayenne pepper and sesame seeds. Set aside until ready to use.

Sear the chicken tenderloins on a chargrill or in a frying pan and, when cooked, roll the tenderloins in the dukkah. Serve with sides of extra virgin olive oil and balsamic glaze.

Prep time: 30 mins   **Cooking time:** 10 mins   **Serves:** 6-8

Chef's tip: Dukkah is an Egyptian blend of nuts and seeds traditionally used for dipping with bread and olive oil. It is easily available ready-made if you don't want to make your own.

To drink: Kirrihill Companions Riesling Pinot Gris, Clare Valley/Adelaide Hills, SA.

bbq squid salad
w sesame + umeboshi plum sauce

3 large squid tubes
500ml milk
2 tablespoons sambal oelek
2 Lebanese cucumbers
1 red capsicum
300g green beans

1 bunch coriander leaves
3 tablespoons umeboshi
   plum sauce
1 tablespoon honey
2 tablespoons sesame oil
75ml mirin

Score the insides of the squid tubes in a crisscross pattern. Cut squid into halves and then cut into 4 cm thick pieces, then soak in milk and sambal oelek for a minimum of 1 hour to soften.

For the salad, slice cucumber into half moons, slice red capsicum and green beans and roughly chop the bunch of coriander leaves. Toss together in a bowl and set aside in the fridge until needed.

With a whisk combine umeboshi plum sauce, honey, sesame oil and mirin until emulsified. Set aside.

Heat up the BBQ then drain the squid and sear on the heat for 2 to 3 minutes or until cooked through. Be careful not to overcook the squid as it will become tough. Toss the dressing through the salad before serving and top the salad with the BBQ squid.

Prep time: 1hr 30 mins   **Cooking time:** 10 mins   **Serves:** 6

Chef's tip: Japanese umeboshi plum sauce is available from Asian grocers and has a uniquely salty/tart flavour. Mirin is similar to sake.

To drink: Shaw Vineyard Estate Riesling, Murrumbateman, NSW.

golden money bags
w chicken + five spice

500g chicken mince
1 bunch coriander,
   finely chopped
1 teaspoon ground ginger
¼ teaspoon white pepper
½ teaspoon five spice powder
1 bunch chives,
   finely chopped

1 teaspoon fish sauce
1 leek
32 square wonton wrappers
   (available at the supermarket)
2 litres peanut oil
16 wooden skewers

In a bowl combine mince, coriander, ginger, white pepper, five spice, chives and fish sauce. Allow to chill in the fridge for 10 minutes. While the mince is chilling, heat a pot of water to boiling, trim the base of the leek and slice off 32 vertical strips, approx ½ cm wide to make lengths to use as ties. Transfer to the boiling water to blanch for 20 seconds, drain and set aside.

Separate wonton wrapper squares and place 1 teaspoon of mince in the middle of the wrapper. Pull the corners into the centre around the mince and pinch together.

Take a piece of leek and wrap around the pinched part of the bundle and tie. Repeat for all 32 pieces.

Heat peanut oil in a deep saucepan until it is hot and sizzling when you place a bundle in the oil. In small batches place the bundles into the oil and fry for approximately 1½ minutes, until golden and crunchy on the outside.

Remove and drain on paper towel. Thread two bundles on each skewer and serve immediately.

Prep time: 30 mins   **Cooking time:** 10 mins   **Makes:** 16 skewers

Chef's tip: These can be served on their own or with your choice of bought sauces such as soy, chilli or plum.

To drink: Tintilla Angus Semillon, Hunter Valley, NSW.

pork belly bites

1.5 kg pork belly, no rib attached
250g table salt
4 tablespoons vegetable oil

Preheat oven to 230°C. Place pork belly skin side up in baking tray on 1 tablespoon of vegetable oil. Rub another tablespoon of vegetable oil on the skin of the pork belly and cover the surface of the skin with all the salt. This will form the crust when cooking.

Place the tray into the hot oven for 15 minutes then reduce the heat to 120°C for a further hour. Remove pork belly from the oven and take off the salt crust. Allow the meat to rest for 15 minutes.

Heat remaining vegetable oil in a non-stick pan and, when it begins to smoke, place the pork belly into the pan skin side down for approximately 1 minute. This will make the skin bubble and crackle. Be careful not to burn the skin. If the skin hasn't completely bubbled, carefully press the skin side down for a further 30 seconds.

Remove from the pan and rest on a board for 5 minutes then cut the meat into bite-sized cubes and serve with toothpicks.

Prep time: 10 mins   **Cooking time:** 1½ hrs   **Serves:** 6-8

Chef's tip: The roasting of the pork belly can be cooked in advance and reheated just before the skin crackling process.

To drink: Rolling Chardonnay, Central Ranges, NSW.

tofu pad thai
w tamarind + lime

1 packet thai-style dry flat noodles
2 tablespoons vegetable oil
4 tablespoons crushed peanuts roasted (optional)
1 tablespoon crushed garlic
1 bunch spring onions, sliced into 4cm slices
250g extra firm tofu, sliced into 4cm slices

2 tablespoons fish sauce
1 tablespoon tamarind paste
1 teaspoon shrimp paste
½ teaspoon chilli powder
1 egg, whisked
½ packet crisp bean shoots
4 tablespoons bought dried fried shallots
6 lime wedges

In a heatproof bowl, soak noodles in boiling water until just soft.

Drain and set aside. Heat 1 tablespoon of vegetable oil in a wok and cook crushed peanuts until golden. Drain and set aside.

Heat the remaining oil in the wok, add garlic, spring onions and tofu and lightly brown. Make sure the wok remains hot and add the drained noodles, tossing until the noodles are hot.

Add fish sauce, tamarind paste, shrimp paste and chilli powder and toss. Move ingredients to the side of the wok to make a space for the egg.

Add egg and cook until almost set. Combine the egg through the rest of the ingredients and toss through the bean sprouts until warm.

Serve topped with peanuts, fried shallots and a wedge of lime.

Prep time: 20 mins   **Cooking time:** 10 mins   **Serves:** 4

Chef's tip: Tamarind and shrimp paste are available at some supermarkets, Asian grocers and gourmet delis.

To drink: Optimiste Chardonnay, Mudgee, NSW.

sticky rice
+ guava parcels

1 cup sticky (glutinous) rice
2 large banana leaves
300ml coconut milk
4 ripe guavas
4 tablespoons light palm sugar

Cover sticky rice in cold water and soak for 2 hours. Soak banana leaves in warm water for 2 hours to soften. Drain rice and place in saucepan with coconut milk and simmer until rice is soft and coconut milk is absorbed, approximately 10-12 minutes. If the rice is still a bit firm you can add small quantities of water until the rice is soft and sticky.

Peel and dice 3 of the guavas and place in a saucepan with palm sugar. Dissolve sugar over a low heat until it starts to caramelise and the fruit is soft. Remove from the heat.

Cut softened banana leaves into 15cm squares. Place 3 tablespoons of sticky rice into the middle of each leaf. Make a well in the middle of the rice and place a tablespoon of the guava into each well and cover over with the rice.

Fold the banana leaf around the rice to make a parcel. Tie with string or strips of remaining banana leaf.

When ready to use, steam the parcels over boiling water in baskets. Alternatively you can reheat the parcels on a BBQ. To serve, break the top of the parcels open and garnish with slices of fresh guava.

Prep time: 35 mins + soaking time   **Cooking time:** 20 mins   **Serves:** 6

Chef's tip: Cheat by buying sticky rice parcels from Chinese bakers or Asian stores – just add guava or other seasonal, tropical fruit. Banana leaf is available at Asian grocers.

To drink: Shaw Vineyard Estate Botrytis Semillon, Murrumbateman, NSW.

live it
up

Think high society, dressing up for the
cocktail hour and delighting your guests
with bite-sized taste sensations.

saucy prawn cocktails
w tabasco

125ml whole egg mayonnaise
2 tablespoons tomato sauce
1 tablespoon lemon juice
1 tablespoon Worcestershire sauce
1 teaspoon Tabasco sauce
8 cooked, peeled Crystal Bay prawns,
   tails on
¼ red cabbage finely shredded
¼ iceberg lettuce finely shredded

In a bowl whisk together whole egg mayonnaise, tomato sauce, lemon juice, Worcestershire sauce and Tabasco sauce.

Take 8 small serving dishes and place a small amount of finely shredded lettuce in 4 of the dishes and finely shredded red cabbage in the other 4. Place a prawn tail up on top of each and a spoon of cocktail sauce. Place in the fridge to chill.

Prep time: 15 mins   **Serves:** 8

Chef's tip: These are also great served on Chinese spoons.

To drink: Blue Pyrenees Brut, Pyrenees, VIC.

wasabi jelly oysters
w ginger + lime

1 dozen fresh-shucked Sydney rock
  oysters (with shells)
1 cup of water
Juice of 1 lime
2 small pieces fresh root ginger
1½ teaspoons powdered gelatine
1 teaspoon wasabi paste
¼ cup fresh coriander leaves
Dry uncooked rice

Remove oysters from their shells and place in a clean container in the fridge. Rinse the insides of the shells to remove any grit. Pat dry and place in the fridge to chill.

In a pan place water, lime juice and ginger, heat and allow to boil for 2 minutes. Place gelatine powder in a mug and add ⅓ cup of the hot lime/ginger juice to the gelatine to dissolve. Pour the mix back into the pan and add the wasabi paste. Remove ginger pieces and discard, then whisk the liquid until the wasabi has dissolved.

Take a flat baking tray and cover with dry rice to form a 'bed' for the oyster shells. Arrange them so they are level and then pour as much of the liquid into the shells as they will hold. Place a couple of coriander leaves in the liquid of each shell then return the shells to the fridge to set the jelly.

When set, remove the shells from the tray, dusting off any rice that may have stuck to the outside of the shells. Arrange the oyster shells on a serving plate, place the oysters on each shell and serve. The oysters will look as if they are floating.

Prep time: 15 mins   **Makes:** 12

To drink: Kirrihill Adelaide Hills Pinot Grigio, Adelaide Hills, SA.

quail eggs
w smoked salmon + caviar

12 quail eggs
4 tablespoons good quality
   mayonnaise
30g jar of black lumpfish caviar
100g smoked salmon slices

Boil quail eggs for 1-1½ minutes, cool in fresh cold water for 5 minutes and then peel.

Combine mayonnaise with 2 tablespoons of caviar and set aside.

Slice salmon into 12 narrow ribbons. Wrap a strip of salmon around each of the eggs, place on a spoon and top with a small spoonful of caviar mayonnaise.

Serve on a plate of crushed ice to keep cool.

Prep time: 10 mins   **Cooking time:** 7 mins   **Makes:** 12

Chef's tip: Caviar can be extremely expensive, black lumpfish caviar is an inexpensive alternative, available from the supermarket.

To drink: Rolling Sparkling Pinot Grigio Chardonnay, Central Ranges, NSW.

chilled vichyssoise
w crème fraiche + chives

3 leeks
250g potatoes, peeled
50g butter unsalted
1.5 litres water
½ bunch thyme, tied with string
½ teaspoon salt
½ teaspoon ground white pepper
½ cup crème fraiche
½ bunch chives finely chopped

Slice the white part of the leeks into ½cm thick rings and dice potato into small cubes. Soften butter in a medium pan, add leeks and sauté without allowing them to brown. Once softened, add the potato, water, thyme, salt and pepper. Bring the pot to the boil and simmer for 30 minutes.

When potatoes are soft, remove from the heat and take out the thyme bundle. Place the leek and potato mix into a blender and purée. When there are no lumps place the purée back into the pot and stir in crème fraiche. Bring the liquid back up to a simmer for 2 minutes. Remove from the heat and cool.

To serve, pour into your favourite soup bowls or glasses and chill for an hour, then garnish with finely chopped chives.

Prep time: 10 mins   **Cooking time:** 40 mins   **Serves:** 6

Chef's tip: The story goes that this soup was made famous by a French chef in America who named it after the town of Vichy near his birthplace in France.

To drink: Shaw Vineyard Estate Riesling, Murrumbateman, NSW.

nori squares
w kingfish

200g medium grain or sushi rice
500ml water
3 tablespoons rice wine vinegar
1 tablespoon mirin
1 teaspoon caster sugar

500g fillet fresh kingfish,
   skin off
8 sheets square nori
Baking tin the same size as
   the nori sheets

Rinse rice under running water in a colander until the water runs clear.

Place rice in a pot with 500ml of water. Bring to the boil and reduce to the lowest heat possible to cook for 10-12 minutes with the lid on. Leave with the heat off for a further 5 minutes.

In a small bowl mix rice wine vinegar, mirin and sugar. With a fork mix the liquid through the rice and set aside in the fridge to cool. Thinly slice vertically through kingfish fillets to make pieces ½cm thick.

Line the baking tin with plastic wrap with enough to hang over the edges of the tin.

Now place a nori sheet on top, then a layer of rice approximately 1cm thick. Follow with another layer of nori, a single layer of kingfish, another layer of rice and a final layer of nori sheet.

Press firmly for a minute and remove from the tin. Cut the pressed nori into nine even squares, set aside. Now make a second nori cake using the same method but in a different order – nori, rice, nori, rice, nori and kingfish slices. Cut into nine even squares and place alternatively on a presentation plate for the best effect.

Prep time: 40 mins   **Cooking time:** 15 mins   **Serves** 6-12

To drink: Climbing Pinot Gris, Orange, NSW.

stilton rolls
w aubergines + field mushrooms

2 aubergines
salt
30ml olive oil
30g butter
1 medium brown onion,
   peeled and diced

2 large field mushrooms,
   diced
200g cream cheese
200g stilton cheese

Slice aubergines lengthways into 6 strips, 2cm wide. Lay them on a clean surface and salt both sides lightly to draw out any bitterness. Wash after 10 minutes and press firmly between sheets of paper towel to dry.

Add olive oil and aubergine strips to a frying pan and fry until browned slightly on both sides. Remove, drain on paper towel and cool. Heat butter in a clean pan, add diced onion and mushrooms and fry until soft and no liquid is left in the pan. Set aside to cool.

In a bowl, beat cream cheese and stilton together until smooth. Lay out the aubergine slices and spread a thin layer of creamed cheese and a thin layer of mushroom and onion. Roll up lengthways and cut in half to form 2 rolls out of each slice of aubergine. Garnish with a green sprout such as sunflower sprouts.

Prep time: 30 mins   **Cooking time:** 10 mins   **Serves:** 12

Chef's tip: If you don't have the time to make your own aubergine slices they are readily available at the supermarket deli section.

To drink: Blue Pyrenees Chardonnay, Pyrenees, VIC.

sweet apple
+ goat's cheese tarts

3 green apples
75g caster sugar
½ teaspoon ground cinnamon
60ml water
200g soft goat's cheese
12 sweet mini tart cases
2 large red delicious apples

Peel, core and dice 2 of the green apples and place in a saucepan with sugar, cinnamon and 60ml of water. Simmer with a lid on for 5 minutes, making sure the pan does not go dry. Mash the apple into a smooth purée and cool.

Place a spoonful of purée into each of the tart cases. Top with goat's cheese and garnish with a thin slice of red apple and diced red and green apple pieces as shown.

Prep time: 15 mins   **Cooking time:** 5 mins   **Serves:** 12

Chef's tip: If you are making these ahead of time, squeeze a little lemon juice over the apple garnish to stop them going brown. You can vary this recipe with other combinations including fig and goat's cheese.

To drink: Kirrihill Companions Riesling Pinot Gris, Clare Valley/Adelaide Hills, SA.

turkish delight
w strawberries + rose petals

4 cups caster sugar
1 litre water
2 teaspoons lemon juice (no pulp)
1 cup cornflour
1 teaspoon cream of tartar
2 drops red food colouring

2 tablespoons of rosewater
3 small strawberries, thinly sliced
optional garnish:
½ cup icing sugar mixture,
   for dusting
edible rose petals*

Mix caster sugar, 2 cups of water and lemon juice in a saucepan. Dissolve sugar over a low heat until there are no crystals remaining, do not boil. Simmer for 5 minutes and remove from the heat.

In another saucepan combine cornflour and cream of tartar with the remaining water to form a smooth paste. Stir with a wooden spoon continuously and bring the mixture to the boil to thicken, then slowly pour the sugar syrup into the cornflour, stirring briskly.

Bring back to a slow simmer and allow the mixture to cook gently, uncovered, for 50 minutes until translucent and golden in colour. Add the food colouring and rosewater and stir to mix well. Remove from the heat and pour into a lightly greased rectangular or square cake tin.

Place the slices of strawberry evenly into the mix so you will have some in each square when you cut later. Cool uncovered for a minimum of 2½ hours or overnight. When you are ready to serve, slice the Turkish delight into even squares using an oiled knife for clean edges. Dust with icing sugar if you like and top with edible rose petals.

Prep time: 10 mins + cooling time   **Cooking time:** 1½ hrs   **Serves:** 8-12

Chef's tip: *The edible rose petals we used are dried and available from gourmet delis. You can also use dried strawberries in place of fresh.

To drink: Douwe Egberts coffee.

yin yang chocolate ganache

500g dark chocolate buttons
500g white chocolate buttons
2/3 cup thickened cream
12 moulds,
    9-10cm wide x 5-6cm high

4 sheets of A4 transparent film
   cut into 12 long strips, 4cm wide
1 pastry brush
1 piping bag
3 sheets gold leaf
12 redcurrants

In separate bowls over hot water, melt 300g of the dark and white chocolate buttons each with 1/3 cup of thickened cream. Stir each until combined and then cool to room temperature.

In a clean bowl melt a further 200g of dark chocolate and use a pastry brush to paint 6 of the transparency strips with three coats of chocolate each. Pick up the furthest end of the strip and bring towards you joining ends together leaving a loop.

Turn the strip on its side and place inside one of the moulds to form the curved, 'tear drop' shape. Repeat the process another 5 times and refrigerate. Do a couple of extras in case some break. Repeat the process with the white chocolate.

When chocolate has set, remove the loop from the mould and carefully peel back the transparent strip. Place the chocolate in a cool place on some baking paper to rest on their sides. Fill the piping bag with the matching thickened chocolate ganache and pipe into the centre of the loops. Carefully scrape the top of the loops with the flat of a spatula or the back of your knife to produce a smooth level top surface. Repeat the process for the white chocolate ganache and loops.

With a cotton bud carefully dab the gold leaf onto the outside of the dark chocolate loops for garnish. Arrange on a plate in the yin yang symbol shape with dark and white combination. Garnish the centres of the loops with a redcurrant.

Prep time: 1 hr   **Cooking time:** 5 mins   **Serves:** 6

Chef's tip: This sounds difficult, but you will see how to make the loops as you follow the steps. Redcurrants are available from supermarkets. Gold leaf is available from specialist food stores.

To drink: Shaw Vineyard Estate Botrytis Semillon, Murrumbateman, NSW.

grand gestures

Dinner parties with a difference
begin with cocktails to set the
mood and flow on through easy courses
that complement conversation.

creamy fettuccine
w pipis + garlic + white wine

1kg pipis
750g fettuccine pasta
2 tablespoons olive oil
1 large brown onion,
   peeled and diced
4 garlic cloves,
   peeled and thinly sliced

1 teaspoon sea salt flakes
125ml cup dry white wine
250ml fish stock
300ml cream
1 bunch chopped flat parsley leaves

Bring a large pot of water to the boil, add a pinch of table salt and cook the fettuccine until tender.

Drain and set aside. In a large saucepan, sauté diced onion in olive oil until soft then add pipis and cover.

Shake the pan to heat the shells evenly for 30 seconds, remove the lid, add the white wine and replace the lid to steam pipis for a further 30 seconds.

When the shells have opened, add garlic and reduce liquid to simmer for another minute but do not allow to dry out.

Add fish stock and bring back to a simmer, add cream and continue to simmer for a further 5 minutes. Place pasta and parsley into the pot with the pipis and toss. Transfer to bowls, spooning the remaining sauce over each serving and sprinkle with a few sea salt flakes.

Prep time: 15 mins   **Cooking time:** 20 mins   **Serves:** 6

To drink: Kirrihill Adelaide Hills Pinot Grigio, Adelaide Hills, SA.

goat's cheese bavarois

w purple basil

4 egg yolks
100g caster sugar
500ml milk
½ teaspoon vanilla essence
200g soft goat's cheese

250ml thickened cream
3 gelatine leaves
1 bunch purple basil
Canola oil spray
8 bavarois moulds

Whisk egg yolks and caster sugar together in bowl until creamy and pale in colour.

In a saucepan bring milk and vanilla to the boil. When hot add crumbled goat's cheese and stir until the mixture is smooth. Remove from the heat and pour slowly over the egg mixture, whisking continuously.

Place mixture back into the saucepan and heat slowly, stirring with a wooden spoon and remove from the heat when thick enough to coat the back of the spoon. Soak gelatine leaves in cool water. When soft, squeeze the leaves in your hand to drain and add to the saucepan. Leave mixture to cool (but not set), add the thickened cream and stir through the mixture using a wooden spoon.

Spray the inside of the moulds with oil then fill almost to the top with bavarois mixture. Pick the best looking basil leaves from the bunch and use the handle end of a clean spoon to push the leaves against the interior sides and onto the base of the moulds. Place in the fridge.

10 minutes later, before the bavarois set, give the leaves another push against the sides of the moulds to make sure they are visible to create the delicate pattern. Refrigerate for a further 40 minutes to an hour to make sure they are set before turning out to serve.

Prep time: 20 mins + setting time   **Cooking time:** 10 mins   **Makes:** 8

 Chef's tip: These can be served as an entrée, savoury dessert or as an accompaniment to a savoury main. Bavarois moulds are available from specialist food stores.

peking duck salad
w papaya + mango chutney

1 BBQ Peking duck
1 ripe papaya
2 bunches of choy sum
250g jar of mango chutney

Preheat oven to 100°C for warming. Divide cooked Peking duck into 2 whole breasts and 2 whole thighs keeping the skin on. Place the pieces on a tray and cover with foil to keep moist. Place in the oven to warm for 10 minutes.

While duck is warming, bring a pot of water to the boil for the choy sum. Peel and de-seed papaya and cut into 12 slices.

Heat papaya on both sides in a non-stick pan to caramelise the natural sugars. Set aside. Cut the root end, about 4cm, off the choy sum and blanch in boiling water for 30 to 40 seconds until the stalks are soft, then drain.

Slice duck breast and thigh meat into 3 pieces each. Place 4 folded bundles of choy sum on each plate and top each with 3 slices of papaya and 3 slices of duck. Serve with a side of mango chutney, slightly warmed if you like.

Prep time: 20 mins   **Cooking time:** 15 mins   **Serves:** 4

Chef's tip: You could go to the effort of cooking your own BBQ duck or, instead, pick up a great duck done by the experts such as BBQ King (Sydney) or your local Chinese BBQ restaurant.

To drink: Optimiste Petit Verdot, Mudgee, NSW.

cajun crab crepes

150g plain flour
250ml milk
pinch salt
1 egg, beaten
1 tablespoon canola oil
1 tablespoon butter

250g crab meat
20g Cajun spice
6 charred peppers
   cut into thin strips
2 avocados, peeled and sliced
125ml crème fraiche

Combine flour, milk, salt and beaten egg in a bowl and whisk until smooth and thin. Stand and rest. Heat butter in a non-stick pan and add the crabmeat and Cajun spice. Toss well to combine spice with crab and remove from the heat when crab is hot.

Heat canola oil in a non-stick crepe pan or shallow frying pan.

Add approximately 3 tablespoons of crepe batter at a time, swirling the pan to make the batter cover the surface.

Cook approximately 30 seconds on either side or until golden.
Repeat the process 5 times.

Preheat oven to 150°C. Fold the crepe over twice to make a triangle.

Open the pocket of the crepe and fill with red pepper strips, avocado slices and crab meat. Reheat the stuffed crepes in the oven for 10 minutes. Garnish with a dollop of crème fraiche and serve.

Prep time: 15 mins   **Cooking time:** 20 mins   **Serves:** 6

To drink: Tintilla Rosato di Jupiter Sangiovese Rosé, Hunter Valley, NSW.

marinated prawn skewers

w sweet peppers

1 lemon, cut into 6 wedges
12 green Crystal Bay prawns,
     peeled & deveined, tails on
6   red and yellow mini peppers
     (3 of each)
1   red onion,
     peeled and cut into 6 wedges

125ml olive oil
Juice of 2 lemons
1 teaspoon sea salt
2 tablespoons crushed garlic
6 long bamboo skewers

Thread 6 skewers with the following: a wedge of lemon, green prawn, red or yellow sweet pepper, another prawn and finish with a wedge of red onion.

Combine olive oil, lemon juice, salt and garlic in a long container that will accommodate the skewers. Soak the threaded skewers in the marinade for a minimum of 1 hour in the fridge to allow the flavours to soak in.

Heat the BBQ and cook skewers on either side until the prawns are cooked and the peppers have softened, then serve.

Prep time: 20 mins   **Cooking time:** 10 mins   **Serves:** 6

Chef's tip: The lemon on the top of the skewers makes a nice dressing if squeezed down over the prawns.

To drink: Kirrihill Adelaide Hills Pinot Grigio, Adelaide Hills, SA.

balsamic bbq lamb
w rocket + mint yoghurt

8 trimmed lamb cutlets
¼ cup olive oil
½ cup dark balsamic vinegar
½ cup plain yoghurt

½ cup rough chopped mint leaves
1 teaspoon Murray River Salt flakes
1 packed cup rocket leaves

Place lamb cutlets in a bowl with the olive oil and balsamic vinegar and marinate for at least an hour in the fridge.

Fire up the BBQ or chargrill plate – use the grill if you don't have either.

In a bowl combine yoghurt and mint leaves and set aside.

Cook lamb cutlets on one side for approximately 1½ minutes only and turn. Cook for a further 1½ minutes and remove from the heat.

Arrange rocket leaves on a plate, add the cooked cutlets, then top with dollops of mint yoghurt and serve.

Prep time: 15 mins   **Cooking time:** 5 mins   **Makes:** 8

Chef's tip: Cooking time for the cutlets depends on their thickness but overcooking can make them dry. Lamb is best served a little pink in the centre to maintain moisture.

To drink: Kirrihill Companions Tempranillo Garnacha, Clare Valley/Adelaide Hills, SA.

savoury cheese tart
w pumpkin + oregano

1   medium jap pumpkin,
      peeled and chopped into
      bit-sized chunks
¼ cup canola oil
Short crust savoury pastry
      to line a 12 x 20cm baking dish
6   eggs
300ml thickened cream

200g grated cheddar cheese
1   teaspoon salt
1   teaspoon cracked black pepper
200g blue cheese,
      cut into chunks
1   large Spanish onion,
      peeled and sliced
Leaves from 1 bunch fresh oregano

Preheat oven to 180°C. Place pumpkin chunks on a baking tray, coat liberally with canola oil and bake in the oven for 30 minutes or until soft and browning around the edges. Remove and allow to cool.

While pumpkin is cooking, line the baking dish with shortcrust pastry and blind-bake* for 10-12 minutes or until the top of the pastry begins to turn a light golden brown. Remove from oven.

In a bowl combine eggs, cream, grated cheddar cheese, salt, pepper and oregano leaves. Next, loosely fill the pastry case in the baking dish with pumpkin pieces. Pour over egg, cream and cheddar cheese mixture until it almost fills the dish and arrange chunks of blue cheese over the top with slices of onion.

Place in the oven to bake for 35 minutes or until the top is golden and the centre springs back when you tap it lightly in the centre. This can be served hot or cold and is a great dish to take on a picnic.

Prep time: 40 mins   **Cooking time:** 35 mins   **Serves:** 6-12

Chef's tip: *Blind-baking the pastry is a method of par-baking used when a filling won't take as long to cook as the pastry itself. To stop the pastry rising at the centre, place a sheet of greaseproof paper over the pastry with some weights on top. If you don't have baking weights, place a cup of dry rice on the greaseproof paper.

To drink: Rolling Chardonnay, Central Ranges, NSW.

blueberry cheese bites

1 packet chocolate ripple biscuits
125g unsalted butter, melted
200g blue cheese
150g Philadelphia cream cheese

¼ cup caster sugar
¼ cup thickened cream
1 punnet fresh blueberries

Place biscuits in a food processor to make biscuit crumbs. Place crumbs into a bowl and pour over melted butter mixing together with a spoon.

Place blue cheese, Philadelphia cheese, caster sugar and cream into a food processor and combine until thick and smooth. Place mixture into a piping bag.

Take a cutter approximately 4-5cm round and line the sides with a tube of baking paper a little higher than the cutter. Press a couple of centimetres of the biscuit base into the cutter and pipe a further few centimetres of cheese mix on top of the biscuit base.

Remove the cutter (but not the paper) by pushing the base up through the cutter and repeat the process a further 5 times.

Place the individual pieces on a tray and place in the fridge to set for 15 minutes.

Remove the paper from the pieces, arrange fresh blueberries on the top of each and transfer to a plate to serve.

Prep time: 35 mins   **Serves:** 6

To drink: Shaw Vineyard Estate Semi Sweet Riesling, Murrumbateman, NSW.

marsala shortbread stacks
w chocolate + toffee topping

1 cup caster sugar
1 cup water
30ml white vinegar
Spray cooking oil
32 round shortbread biscuits

220ml thickened cream
2 drops vanilla essence
50g block dark cooking chocolate
500ml Marsala wine*

Toffee filigree toppings are a party showpiece and very easy to do. In a small pan bring the caster sugar, water and vinegar to the boil and continue until the water evaporates and the sugar starts to turn a light golden colour.

Remove from the heat and allow the hot sugar to stand and cool slightly until it will slowly slide off a wooden spoon in a steady stream. Spray a baking tray size sheet of greaseproof paper with cooking oil and drizzle toffee to create a web shape approximately 10cm wide to form the decoration for the top of each stack.

Repeat the process to make 8 webs in total. When the toffee has hardened, remove from the greaseproof paper and store in an airtight container with greaseproof paper layered between each toffee web so they don't stick. Keep in a cool place.

In a bowl whip cream and vanilla essence to form stiff peaks. Place the Marsala in a separate bowl, dip (but don't soak) each biscuit separately in Marsala and place a teaspoon of whipped cream on top. Repeat the process three times layering cream and biscuits on top of each other to form a stack. Refrigerate the stacks until you are ready to serve.

To serve, grate dark chocolate over the top of each stack and carefully place a toffee filigree web on the top.

Prep time: 30 mins   **Cooking time:** 10 mins   **Serves:** 8

Chef's tip: *Marsala is a fortified wine from the Marsala region in Sicily, similar to Port.

To drink: Tintilla Edwardo Fortified Semillon, Hunter Valley, NSW.

crowd
pleasers

Meet up at your place before a game or whenever there's an excuse to gather friends together and serve satisfying food that scores top marks every time.

pizza fingers
w sweet chilli chicken or pepperoni

sweet chilli chicken fingers

2 x 10" bought pizza bases
6 chicken tenderloins
1 tablespoon canola oil
¼ cup sweet chilli sauce
6 baby corn stalks
¼ cup canned water chestnuts,
   drained and sliced
2 tablespoons fried shallots
   (available at the supermarket
   or Asian grocer)
3 sprigs of fresh coriander

pepperoni fingers

2 x 10" bought pizza bases
2 tablespoons olive oil
2 stalks fresh thyme
½ teaspoon crushed garlic
120g tub tomato paste
½ red onion,
   peeled and finely sliced
9 slices pepperoni
100g blue cheese,
   crumbled
1 deli-style chargrilled red
   capsicum, sliced
¼ cup shaved Parmesan

Preheat oven to 180°C. Trim each pizza base into 3 rectangular fingers to make 12.

Sweet chilli chicken fingers: Lightly fry chicken tenderloins in canola oil, slice and set aside. Spread sweet chilli sauce evenly over 6 of the pizza base fingers then add water chestnut slices, cooked chicken tenderloins, baby corn, fried shallots and fresh coriander.

Pepperoni fingers: Mix olive oil, leaves of thyme stalks, garlic and tomato paste in a bowl. Spread the mix evenly over the remaining 6 pizza bases. Top with sliced red onion, pepperoni, blue cheese, capsicum strips and Parmesan cheese.

Place all fingers on a greased oven tray and bake for 10 minutes or until the toasted.

Prep time: 25 mins   **Cooking time:** 10 mins   **Makes:** 12

To drink: Rolling Sauvignon Blanc Semillon, Central Ranges, NSW.

southern fried chicken
w cayenne + oregano

8 chicken drumsticks
1 litre buttermilk
2 tablespoons Tabasco sauce
3 cups flour
1 tablespoon salt
2 tablespoons garlic powder

2 tablespoons onion powder
1 tablespoon cayenne pepper
2 tablespoons sweet paprika
2 tablespoons dried oregano
1½-2 litres canola oil
8 lemon wedges

Soak drumsticks in buttermilk and Tabasco sauce in a covered bowl for a minimum of 1 hour or, preferably, overnight.

In a bowl, sieve together flour, salt, garlic powder, onion powder, cayenne pepper, sweet paprika and dried oregano. Roll drumsticks in the seasoned flour mix to coat, dip each one into the buttermilk and then roll a second time in the flour mix.

Heat oil in a heavy-based, high sided frying pan or deep saucepan – you need enough so that when you add the chicken drumsticks the oil will come half way up the side of each piece. Place drumsticks in the hot oil and fry for 8-10 minutes each side until golden and crunchy. Drain on paper towel and serve with some lemon wedges.

Prep time: 20 mins + marinating time   **Cooking time:** 16-20 mins   **Serves:** 8

black quinoa bean salad
w apricots + figs

1 cup adzuki beans*
1 cup black or red quinoa*
4 cups of water
2 tablespoons seeded grain mustard
1 tablespoon honey
60ml white wine vinegar
60ml olive oil

60ml apricot nectar
1 red onion,
    peeled and finely diced
1 cup sliced dried Turkish apricots
1 cup semi-dried figs,
    roughly chopped

Place dried adzuki beans in a bowl of cold water and soak overnight.

When ready to use, rinse the quinoa grains in a sieve under running water for 2 minutes. Using 2 separate pans, add 2 cups of water to each. Heat to bring the first to the boil, add quinoa and boil rapidly for 10 minutes before straining and cooling. Meanwhile, add adzuki beans to the second pan of water, bring to the boil and reduce the heat to simmer for 15 minutes. Strain and cool.

In a bowl combine seeded mustard, honey, white wine vinegar, olive oil and apricot nectar. Whisk until all ingredients combine to make a dressing.

In another bowl combine quinoa, adzuki beans, diced red onion, Turkish apricots and figs and toss to combine. Pour half the dressing over the salad and transfer to a serving bowl. Pour the remaining dressing over the salad before serving.

Prep time: 10 mins   **Cooking time:** 15 mins   **Serves:** 8-12

Chef's Tip: *Quinoa (pr. keen-wah) is a native of the South American Andes with edible seeds which have a nutty flavour a bit like wild rice and come in a variety of colours. Available at supermarkets – look at the health food section – and health food stores such as Macro Wholefoods. Likewise *adzuki beans, which also have a nutty flavour and combine beautifully with the quinoa.

To drink: Optimiste Chardonnay, Mudgee, NSW.

sumac crusted beef
w tomato chilli jam + couscous

2 long beef fillets*
3 tablespoons olive oil
45g ground sumac*
250g jar tomato chilli jam

2 cups couscous
2 cups hot water
1 tablespoon vegetable oil
½ cup semi-dried cranberries

Preheat the oven to 180°C. Heat oil in a pan and, when it starts to smoke, place the fillet into the pan and sear until golden brown on all sides.

When seared, remove fillet from the pan, roll in the sumac then return to the pan and place in the oven.

If your pan does not have an ovenproof handle, transfer the fillet to a separate roasting tray. Roast in the oven for 12 minutes then remove and allow to sit for a further 10 minutes to rest.

Place couscous in a pan, add hot water, cover and leave to stand for 5 minutes. Add the oil and cranberries, fluff with a fork, then transfer to a serving plate.

Slice the beef into 2cm slices and arrange on top of the couscous.

Top with spoonfuls of tomato chilli jam to serve.

Prep time: 10 mins   **Cooking time:** 30 mins   **Serves:** 8-12

Chef's tip: *Australia has some of the best beef in the world and a long fillet is one of the finest cuts. The cut has a thin end and thick end – for the same thickness you can ask your butcher to join 2 fillets thick end to thin end and bind together. Alternatively cook them separately so the thick end will be rare while the thin end will be pounced on by those who desire medium to well-done! *Sumac is a deep red, Middle Eastern spice used to add a unique, lemony taste, you'll find it in the herbs and spices section at the supermarket.

To drink: Blue Pyrenees Cabernet Sauvignon, Pyrenees, VIC.

bbq garfish
w chilli + babaganoush

6 whole garfish, cleaned
1 teaspoon chilli paste
1 teaspoon sweet paprika
75ml olive oil

babaganoush
1 aubergine
75ml tahini
3 teaspoons crushed garlic
75ml lemon juice
½ teaspoon ground cumin
pinch salt and pepper
olive oil to cook

Preheat the flat plate of the BBQ on medium setting. Combine the chilli paste, paprika and 75ml olive oil to form a paste, then coat both sides of the garfish and marinade in the fridge until ready to cook.

To make the babaganoush, slice the aubergine in half and roast, skin side down on a baking tray in the oven for 30 minutes. Remove from the oven and scoop the soft flesh from the inside of both halves into a mixing bowl. Add tahini, garlic, lemon juice, cumin and a pinch each of salt and pepper. Mix together with a hand blender until smooth. Place into a serving bowl and refrigerate until ready to use.

Add a little olive oil to the flat plate of the BBQ, add the garfish and cook for no more than 1½ minutes each side as it is a very delicate thin fish. Drain onto paper towel before placing on a serving plate. Serve with babaganoush.

Prep time: 10 mins   **Cooking time:** 30 mins   **Serves:** 6

Chef's tip: If you don't want to make your own babaganoush of course you can buy a good quality brand at your local deli. You can also pan-fry the garfish – they are very delicate, so be careful not to overcook.

To drink: Kirrihill Adelaide Hills Pinot Grigio, Adelaide Hills, SA.

spicy lamb kofta
w coriander + orange

2 tablespoons ground cumin

1 teaspoon ground chilli

1 tablespoon ground caraway seeds

1 tablespoon crushed fenugreek
   seeds

2 tablespoons garam masala

4 garlic cloves,
   peeled and crushed

1 teaspoon cracked black pepper

1 teaspoon salt

2 medium brown onions,
   peeled and diced

½ cup of canola oil

2kg lamb mince

2 eggs beaten

1 cup roughly chopped coriander
   leaves

Grated zest of 2 oranges

½ cup breadcrumbs

2 oranges sliced

500ml orange juice

500ml crushed tomatoes

In a large bowl combine cumin, ground chilli, crushed caraway seeds, crushed fenugreek seeds, garam masala, crushed garlic, black pepper and salt. Heat a non-stick pan with ¼ cup canola oil and sauté diced onion until lightly golden then add spices, stirring with a wooden spoon for a further 2 minutes on a low heat without burning.

Place lamb mince in another large bowl with spice mix, beaten egg, coriander, orange zest and breadcrumbs. Mix with your hands until ingredients are well combined. Roll mixture into 16 separate balls, 130g each. Heat remaining oil in the non-stick pan, add the balls and fry to seal the outsides, then place them into a baking dish a few centimetres higher than the height of the balls.

Preheat the oven to 180°C. Mix the crushed tomato and orange juice together and pour over balls. Place slices of orange randomly in between the balls then cover with foil and cook in the oven for 30 minutes.

When cooked, arrange the balls on a large serving plate (a pyramid looks good) and pour a desired amount of the sauce over the top. Serve as a main dish to share with rice and salads or provide short skewers beside the plate for easy party food.

Prep time: 20 mins   **Cooking time:** 50 mins   **Makes:** 16

To drink: Shaw Vineyard Estate Cabernet Merlot, Murrumbateman, NSW.

corella toffee pears

6 small Corella pears
   (with nice skins)
6 paddle pop sticks
1 cup of water
2 cups caster sugar
30ml white vinegar

Clean and dry the surface of the pears then make a small slit in the top of the pears and push a paddle pop stick halfway into each pear.

Combine the water, sugar and vinegar in a heavy based saucepan.

Bring to the boil and simmer for approximately 15 minutes or until the toffee reaches a hard cracking stage which you can test by dipping a spoon into the toffee and then placing it into a glass of cold water. When cooled, the toffee should not be sticky and will crack off the spoon. It is advisable to watch toffee syrup continuously to make sure it doesn't burn.

Once the toffee starts to go a light golden colour remove from the heat immediately and dip the pears into the toffee making sure that you coat them all the way to the base of the sticks. Cool at room temperature on a baking tray lined with greaseproof paper.

Prep time: 5 mins   **Cooking time:** 20 mins   **Serves:** 6

Chef's tip: Using a wet pastry brush, wipe the sides of the saucepan to keep sugar crystals from building up. To clean the pan and spoons, fill the pot with water and boil to dissolve any unused toffee.

To drink: Tintilla Edwardo Fortified Semillon, Hunter Valley, NSW.

happy
hour

Impress your guests with
charismatic cocktails,
courtesy of Vibe Hotels.

vibrant days
wild berry fizz

120ml Rolling Chardonnay
45ml Chambord
3 raspberries
4 blueberries
soda water
garnish:
fresh berries

Pour wine into a long beer glass.
Add a little ice and fruit. Add liqueur.
Top up with soda water and ice.
Garnish and serve.

strawberry cooler

120ml Blue Pyrenees Chardonnay
45ml strawberry liqueur
¼ fresh orange
2 strawberries halved
soda water
garnish:
cut strawberry and orange wheel

Pour wine into a long beer glass.
Add a little ice and fruit. Add liqueur.
Top up with soda water and ice.
Garnish and serve.

each recipe makes 1 cocktail

cosmo
perfect balance

pomegranate cosmo:
45ml vodka
15ml Parma pomegranate liqueur
30ml pink grapefruit juice

Pour ingredients into a shaker.
Add ice and shake well. Wet the rim
of the martini glass, dip into caster
sugar. Strain mix into glass.

swanky cosmo (variation):
45ml tequila
15ml Grand Marnier
30ml cranberry juice
½ lime
garnish:
1 lime wheel

Pour ingredients into a shaker.
Add ice and shake well. Strain into a
tall martini glass. Cut a wheel from
the ½ lime for garnish. Squeeze the
remainder into the glass.

the bellini
peachy sparkler

2 white peaches, peeled
   and de-stoned
1 raspberry
dry sparkling wine

Muddle the peaches and raspberry
in a mixer. Double strain into a
champagne flute. Top up with
sparkling wine.

note: a little cherry juice can be
substituted for raspberry. The idea
is to give the drink a pink glow.

bartender's tip: muddling is a
mashing technique used to extract
the flavour from fresh ingredients
either using the muddler on the
back of a bar spoon or a long pestle.

each recipe makes 1 cocktail

caipiroska
cutting edge cool

8 lime wedges
1 teaspoon sugar
15ml sugar syrup
60ml vodka
crushed ice
garnish: none

Muddle 4 lime wedges, sugar and sugar syrup in a cocktail shaker. Add vodka and shake well then strain into an 'old fashioned' glass fill with crushed ice and the other 4 wedges.

under the bridge
smooth and spicy

½ peeled banana
pinch cinnamon
45ml Maker's Mark bourbon
30ml Pimms
ice cubes
garnish: sprinkle of cinnamon

Muddle banana and cinnamon in a shaker. Add alcohol and ice. Shake well. Strain into a martini glass. Garnish and serve.

little collins lychee mule
classic with a kick

60ml vodka
20ml lychee syrup
4   peeled and pitted lychees
4   mint leaves
splash of real (ie cloudy)
    ginger beer

Muddle peeled lychees and mint leaves in a tall straight glass. Add lychee syrup. Add ice and pour in vodka. Stir briskly while adding ginger beer to top up.
garnish: mint sprig

deluxe moscow mule

60ml vodka
10ml lime juice
10ml Cointreau
splash of real (ie cloudy)
    ginger beer

Mix the lemon juice with Cointreau in a tall straight glass. Add ice, pour in vodka. Stir briskly while adding ginger beer to top up.
garnish: none

The classic Moscow Mule contains vodka and ginger beer, a little uninspired maybe, but with the addition of a citrus mix it comes alive.

phillip island iced tea
long, tall and tempting

15ml vodka
15ml gin
15ml white rum
15ml tequila
25ml lemon juice
dash of blue curacao

¾ fill a tall straight glass with ice. Pour in alcohol. Stir briskly while adding lemon juice. Add a dash of blue curacao for colour.
garnish: lemon slice

each recipe makes 1 cocktail

bondi blast
wave of fresh tastes

ice
30ml Finlandia Vodka
15ml Chambord
15ml Paraiso
60ml pineapple juice
splash lemonade
garnish: wheel of lime
    mounted on rim

Place ice in a shaker.
Add alcohol and pineapple juice.
Shake vigorously. Pour all into a
glass. Top up with lemonade.
Garnish and serve.

sex on the park
berry liaison

½ lime, quartered
15ml strawberry liqueur
10ml sugar syrup
crushed ice
30ml Finlandia vodka
15ml Absolut Pepper
60ml cranberry juice
splash lemonade
4 strawberries
    (1/2 reserved for garnish)
garnish: with half a strawberry
    on the rim, optional mint sprig

Muddle the lime, strawberry
liqueur and sugar syrup in shaker,
pressing with a hot spoon. Add ice,
alcohol and cranberry juice, shake
vigorously. Pour all ingredients
into a cosmo glass, top up with
lemonade.

each recipe makes 1 cocktail

vibetini
martini madness

2 lychees, peeled and pitted
5ml sugar syrup
crushed ice
60ml 42° Below vodka
dash Midori
garnish: caster sugar for glass

Muddle lychees and sugar syrup in a shaker. Add ice, pour in alcohol and shake well. Wet the rim of a martini glass, dip into caster sugar. Strain the contents of the shaker into the glass.

Vibetini is an exotic twist on the classic dry martini. There are many stylish variations, with James Bond's Vesper as possibly the most famous.

007's vesper:
75mm lemon peel,
    twisted to release the oils
ice cubes
45ml Gordon's gin
15ml Stolichnaya vodka
1 tablespoon Lillet Blanc

Drop lemon peel into the martini glass. Fill the mixer 2/3 full with ice. Add alcohol. Stir or shake gently. Strain into a martini glass. Garnish and serve.

curvito
get ready to rumba

1 lime
4 mint leaves
1 teaspoon brown sugar
20ml sugar syrup
crushed ice
60mls Havana Club rum
splash lemonade
garnish: mint sprig

Quarter the lime, remove pith. Muddle lime with mint leaves. Add brown sugar and sugar syrup. Fill glass with ice, pour over the rum and shake vigorously. Pour into a cosmo glass. Top up with lemonade.

coffee cocktails

espresso martini

50ml vodka
10ml vanilla liqueur
30ml Piazza d'Oro Espresso
sugar syrup to taste

Pour the alcohol over ice in a shaker. Add coffee and sugar syrup to taste. Shake vigorously to form a thick crème, then strain in to chilled martini glass.

espresso margarita

30ml gold tequila
15ml Kahlúa
15ml Grand Marnier
30ml Piazza d'Oro Espresso
sugar syrup to taste
garnish: rim chilled margarita glass with the sugar-coffee mix using Grand Marnier to stick 4 parts sugar to 1 part coffee

Pour the alcohol over ice in a shaker. Add coffee and sugar syrup to taste. Shake vigorously to form thick crème, then strain in to chilled margarita glass.

pear espresso

30ml Piazza d'Oro Espresso
30ml gold tequila
15ml pear liqueur
15ml Grand Marnier
¼ of a pear
sugar syrup to taste
(amaretto optional)

Muddle pear then add with the remaining ingredients to ice in a shaker. Shake and double strain to removing all pear chunks. Pour into shot glasses.
tip: poach pears beforehand in amaretto and a little water for added flavour.

each recipe makes 1 cocktail

winged keel
exotic undercurrents

2 limes, 1 quartered
1 heaped teaspoon sugar
10ml sugar syrup
ice
30ml Malibu rum
15ml 42° Below vodka
60ml pineapple juice
garnish:
lime slice

Muddle lime quarters, sugar and sugar syrup in a shaker. ¾ fill with ice. Pour over the alcohol and pineapple juice. Shake vigorously and strain into a martini glass. Float a lime slice to garnish and serve.

kings x-rated
red light delight

ice
30ml 42° Below vodka
30ml peach schnapps
160ml cranberry juice
garnish:
mint sprig

Add ice to cosmo glass, pour over the alcohol, swirl. Top up with cranberry juice. Garnish and serve.

each recipe makes 1 cocktail

who
what...

...where?

sydney
designed to inspire

Natural beauty, a rich blend of cultures, energy and appetites make the harbour city a hub of creativity, innovation and entertaining options. Let your urge for harbourside wining and dining flow with these hints from **Sydney-insiders.**

- Indulge in fresh tastes at **Vibe Hotel's Curve Restaurant.**

- Stock up on seafood at **Sydney Fish Markets, Blackwattle Bay;** the world's second largest seafood market outside of Japan.

- Pick-up your produce at the **Growers' Market, Pyrmont** on the first Saturday of the month.

- Enjoy gelato by the **beach at Bondi.**

- **Get a rush and a room at Vibe Hotel North Sydney,** just a few minutes' walk from Luna Park and complete with stunning harbourside views.

- **Feed your culture** with a Sydney Theatre Company performance. Why not join other theatre goers at the Hickson Road Bistro for some pre-performance fare?

- **Visit Macro Wholefoods Market s in Crows Nest** for over 8,000 organic and wholefood products.

- **Pack a picnic** and head to Rushcutters Bay Park on any sunny Sunday.

- Say 'Kampai' to the sake sommelier at **Toko in Surry Hills...** pure Zen!

- Chow down **Yum Cha at Chinatown** over brunch/lunch.

- **Let the Spanish Quarter liven you up,** an 80 metre stretch of pizzazz, paella and flamenco. The Tapas are a great way to feast with your sangria long into the night.

- **Name your poison at the Paddington Inn...** whether it's fashion, food, fine wines, beers or cocktails, the 'Paddo Inn', near Oxford Street, will impress.

- **Experience Sydney in a sip at Opera Bar.** Described as the 'best beer garden in the world', it has unrivalled views of Sydney's jewels - the Opera House, the Harbour Bridge and the Harbour itself.

- Knock back a **C-S Cowboy at Cocklebay Wharf.**

- Lick your fingers clean after scoffing 'light-as-air flathead and chips served in a paper cone' at **Fish Face in Darlinghurst.**

- Fire up with a fiery 'mekong mary' or kick back with a 'lemongrass martini' at **jimmy liks, nestled in the leafy streets of Potts Point.**

- Re-visit Australia's heritage at **The Lord Dudley Hotel, an old English style pub in Woollahra** where you can knock back a beer on the sidewalk with the locals of the inner-east.

- Dine alfresco at **Darling Harbour, King Street Wharf or Cockle Bay Wharf** along the waterfront and try to coincide with a free open-air concert.

- **Recline by the roof-top pool at Vibe Hotel Sydney or Vibe Hotel Rushcutters,** complete with a cocktail in hand.

vibehotels.com.au

melbourne
a mecca for mingling

Melbourne's melting pot of cultures is reflected in a dizzying spread of restaurants, cafes, bistros and bars. Enjoy afternoon tea in the genteel surroundings of a nineteenth-century hotel like Vibe Savoy, watch the world go by in the buzzing laneway cafes or explore a little further.

- Consider your options over a **great coffee at Vibe Hotel Carlton's Curve Cafe.**

- **Time a picnic with a twilight Moonlight Cinema screening** at the Royal Botanic Gardens during the warmer months.

- **Gather a group of friends and hit the shops for a weekend away.** Stay at **Vibe Hotel Savoy Melbourne** for stylish and hip rooms just a couple of blocks from the hub of the city.

- **Learn how to cook 'delizioso' risotto** from the Italian masters themselves at Enotica's Italian Cooking School in Carlton....Buon appetito!

- **Kick back for a Sunday session** or check out **live music at The Esplanade Hotel,** known as 'the Espy' in St Kilda, an Aussie icon for more than 100 years.

- **Get cheap and cheerful Vietnamese** in Victoria Street, Richmond.

- Allow the aroma to seduce and **catch the coffee buzz at Degraves Espresso Bar** – after all, Melbourne is the coffee capital of Australia.

- **Stroll along Acland Street, St Kilda** and salivate over the incredible spread of cakes, pastries and other gourmet delights.

- **Chow down some churros at MoVida Bar de Tapas,** the "best Spanish restaurant in the country."

- **Take the World's Longest Lunch or learn the secrets of top winemakers and chefs** at the Melbourne Food and Wine Festival, held in March each year.

- **Head back in time at '1806',** a cocktail bar named after the year the word 'cocktail' first appeared in print in New York. The impressive cocktail list includes at least one drink for every decade from 1806 to now...

- **Giggle 'til you gag at the Melbourne International Comedy Festival,** held in early April each year.

- Lose yourself in the **Queen Victoria Markets, a colourful, sprawling mass** offering everything from just-caught fish and freshly picked vegetables.

- Pick up the freshest of **fresh produce and deli goods at Prahan Markets** every Tuesday, Thursday, Friday and Saturday.

- **Take a trip to the Yarra Valley and taste stunning pinot noir,** chardonnay and sparkling at vineyards including Domain Chandon and Chateau Yering.

- **Kick back at the end of the day at Vibe Savoy Hotel Melbourne, and sip on a cocktail** in the beautiful art deco heritage building.

vibehotels.com.au

gold coast
glitz, glamour and more

Think beaches and bikinis, glitz and glamour and then beyond – you'll soon learn that 'the Goldie' is also a hub for outdoor entertaining and a gold mine for fresh produce with everything from soft shell crabs and goat's cheese to locally bred Wagyu beef and award winning wines.

- Immerse yourself in the Goldie and **stay at Vibe Hotel Gold Coast,** right in the midst of the hustle and bustle, glitz and glamour.

- Kick back poolside with a **cocktail from Vibe's Curve Bar.**

- Get your fresh food fix at the **Gold Coast Organic Farmer's Markets, Miami** on Sundays.

- **Catch a spellbinding beach view with true Aussie flavour** at the Northcliffe Life Saving Club.

- **Dance 'til you drop at Melbas** on Cavill Ave, one of the most popular night spots on the Coast.

- **Step into the set of the 'Australian Outback Spectacular' extravaganza** between Warner Bros Movie World and Wet n' Wild, and enjoy an Aussie BBQ served during the show.

- **Catch some cabaret at Dracula's** at Broadbeach – a two-hour dinner show with music, dance, illusion and comedy.

- Head to the hills and **discover chocolate to die for at The Chocolate Kingdom,** Mt Tamborine.

- **Be seen** in one of the many cafes and bars on Tedder Avenue, Main Beach.

- **Take a cheese-making class** at Witches Chase Cheese Company, Mt Tamborine.

- Pre-order a **gourmet picnic pack and kick back to live jazz** on Sunday afternoons at O'Reilly's Canungra Valley Vineyards, Canungra.

- **Catch a crab and feed the pelicans** on a Mud Crab Cruise on the beautiful Broadwater.

- **Suss out the secrets of tea-making** at Australia's only sub-tropical tea plantation, Madura Tea Estates, Murwillumbah.

- The **Tamborine Mountain Distillery is a liquor aficionado's dream.** Over 60 liquors, schnapps and spirits will put your taste buds into a spin.

- **Take a long lunch at 'Songbirds in the Forest'** on Tamborine Mountain, Queensland's multi-award winning restaurant of the year.

vibehotels.com.au

darwin
laid-back taste of the tropics

Darwin radiates a laid-back, cosmopolitan, tropical atmosphere which draws inspiration from its Asian neighbours and traditional land owners. Discover markets and festivals, Asian cuisine, spectacular sunsets, a massive natural harbour and warm weather all year round.

174

- Feel the vibe at Vibe Hotel Darwin, right on the waterfront. Watch beautiful, privately-owned boats and cruise ships pass through to the sea while sampling one (or more) Curve Bar cocktails.

- Dine in style, harbour-side at Curve Restaurant, Vibe Hotel Darwin.

- Settle under the coconut palms, watch the sunset and choose from a myriad of tantalising aromas flowing from the various food-stalls at the Mindil Beach Sunset Market on Thursday and Sunday nights during the dry season.

- Live a little and indulge in fresh local Northern Territory produce like mud crabs, barramundi, buffalo, kangaroo and crocodile.

- Devour a platter of local seafood at Stokes Hill wharf with a glass of Sauvignon Blanc while watching a cracking good storm between December and February.

- Immerse yourself in the electric atmosphere of the pubs and nightclubs on Mitchell Street where people come worldwide to start their outback tours...you'd be silly not to join them. Access Kakadu, Katherine Gorge or even take a tour across to Broome.

- Head to Casuarina Coastal Reserve in the city's north and take a walk along the beach, catch a sunset from the Dripstone Cliffs or enjoy a picnic.

- Recline in a deckchair, catch whiffs of frangipani and watch an A-grade movie under the stars at the Deckchair Cinema. Hint: take some fish and chips and grab a drink from the bar.

- Wash down delicious Asian, Moroccan and European offerings with a selection from the excellent range of wines or the 20-odd ales on tap at Deck Bar on Mitchell St where the locals meet.

- Take a deep sea fishing tour...or opt for Top End seafood served alfresco at one of the many eateries at the Wharf.

- Take your catch to the big backyard of Litchfield National Park – just one and a half hours from Darwin and be simply spellbound by the lush monsoon forests, waterfalls and rockholes.

Piazza d'Oro Espresso is roasted locally by Douwe Egberts Coffee.

Since 1753, Douwe Egberts has maintained a tradition of selecting, blending and roasting only the finest coffee beans to create an exceptional range of coffees, each with its own unique and distinctive flavour.

wineries

Wines from these vineyards have been matched with recipes throughout Vibe Entertains.

Cumulus Wines

Dedicated cool climate winegrowers in the beautiful rolling hills near Orange, in the Central Ranges of NSW. Cool nights and dry, sunny days enable Cumulus to grow grapes of extremely high quality and character.

The Rolling and Climbing wines, produced from classic grape varieties patiently nurtured in the rich red soils, have distinct varietal characteristics, bringing you the enjoyment of bright, intense fruit, superb length of flavour and elegant structure.

Kirrihill Wines

Innovative and environmentally sound, the winery is located in the gently rolling hills of South Australia's famous Clare Valley. Kirrihill is fortunate to work with a dedicated team of growers who provide grapes for two ranges, the Single Vineyard Series and Companions from two of Australia's finest cool climate regions, the Clare Valley and the Adelaide Hills.

Optimiste Wines

Optimiste hand pick fruit from their estate vineyards in the hills of Mudgee NSW.

Growing conditions allow intense varietal flavours to develop slowly and fully here and the well drained, north facing gravel slopes produce some of the best and cleanest fruit in the district.

Reflecting the brand's name, Cabernet and Petit Verdot in particular are showing great hope and confidence in the Optimiste vineyards.

Blue Pyrenees Estate

was among the modern Australian wine industry's first ventures into cool climate viticulture in Victoria.

Ample amounts of sunshine ensure the grapes ripen to full maturity with the heat moderated by high altitude vineyards (575m) and southerly ocean winds. Essentially, the climate is warm enough to give concentration and power, yet cool enough to give vibrancy and elegance, resulting in remarkable wines from Cabernet Sauvignon, Shiraz, Merlot, Chardonnay and Sauvignon Blanc.

Shaw Vineyard Estate

is located on the historic "Olleyville" property in Murrumbateman, near Canberra, renowned for its Riesling, Semillon, Merlot, Cabernet Sauvignon and Shiraz.

This family owned vineyard is elevated at around 640m, higher than most other vineyards in the Murrumbateman area, which helps mitigate against potential frost damage by allowing good air drainage over the property.

Tintilla Estate

is a family run, 25 acre vineyard in Pokolbin in the heart of the Hunter wine growing area.

Olive trees and woods flank the vineyard with its mosaic of vines planted to match the soils and slopes of the property, creating the unique terroir that produces distinctive, individual, award winning vines. Careful attention to the vineyard produces healthy grapes with optimal ripeness and varietal character.

Low yielding vines produce rich and concentrated fruit with the acidity and tannins that lead to longevity with a softness derived from the Hunter climate.

vibe hotels

thanks

Cookery books
need a team of
people to produce
them and Vibe
Entertains has been a
wonderful example of a
great team effort.